Memories

of

St Albans

The publishers would like to thank the following companies
for their support in the production of this book

Main Sponsor
Pearce Recycling

C & S Dumpleton

St Albans High School for Girls

St Albans School

First published in Great Britain by True North Books Limited
England HX5 9AE

ISBN 1 903204 23 2

Text, design and origination by True North Books Limited
Printed and bound in Great Britain

Memories

of

St Albans

Contents

Introduction

Whenever we meet someone for the first time we go through a ritual exchange of questions. The first information is our name, closely followed by our place of origin, and thirdly by our occupation. Until we identify common points and shared experiences, our personal histories are closely and defensively protected. As we converse and discover links the world becomes a smaller place. Friendships are found to be mutual. We find that we have each trodden the same ground.

As the photograph albums are brought from the drawer, the common bonds are cemented. Each adds a little more knowledge and a few more shared memories. Even if the bonds are not those of blood relatives, the fact that we share common knowledge prompted by the images on the photographs is sufficient to establish a sense of being related. Those memories place us in the history of our home towns and families. We take strength from our honourable ancestry. We develop pride in our communities. Even our accent becomes the best, and other characteristics are imagined that are mutual owing to our backgrounds

For those who live in St Albans the history of their city is well documented, and forever present wherever they go into the city. They have a share in the necessary changes that take place, but the people of St Albans have always sensitively protected their precious heritage. Where the old has been totally obliterated by the establishment of the new, reminders of what went before is preserved in the very names chosen. The shopping precinct, with its offices and library as well as shops, bears the name 'The Maltings'. The Civic Centre Complex with its Law Courts, Police station, Health and Education Centres contains a fine Roman mosaic and other signs that, whilst taking pride in the new the old is still respected and valued.

Continued overleaf

A wartime view of the girls from the Ballito factory posing in an uncomfortable workroom

From previous page
Many street names remind us of their history. As we walk along the elevated pavements of Fishpool Street, admiring the fine domestic architecture there, we are reminded of the right that the people had to fish the Abbey Lake and ponds. The name of the Saxon borough of Kingsbury was preserved by Royal decree. The Royal Borough of Kingsbury was overtaken by the growing market town, as the Abbott encouraged the people to settle in what is now St Albans.

The city welcomes visitors, and proudly displays its heritage on information plaques and boards in all parts of the city. Free tours of the City are offered every Saturday throughout the summer months and people gather in groups at the foot of the historic Clock tower to meet their guide. The Old Town Hall has now been turned over to the important task of giving Tourist Information.

Market days are famous in the city, but today cattle do not wander freely in St Peter's Street, but neither do

This 1960s view is of the railway bridge in Victoria Road, dominated by the Trinity Church, standing on the corner of Beaconsfield Road.

the pedestrians without the help of the crossings. There is always an awareness of the position of the city in the world, not only because the tourists come from all quarters to see this historic city, but because St Albans has always stood at the junction of major highways. Even in ancient times the town of Verulamium was an important link on that Roman road which is known as Watling Street. The London Road collides with Holywell Hill and Chequer Street with as much confusion now as it did when stage-coaches negotiated the corner. They broke their

journeys to Holyhead and other parts, whilst they rested their horses and passengers in the many inns in that area. We can still enjoy the hospitality of the many inns that have survived the changes that have occured through time.

Many industries have grown and died in St Albans. The people, whilst fiercely proud of their past, do not wish their city to become a living museum. They can look back on its proud history whilst keeping their eyes towards the future.

St Albans Central Library

Street scenes

The chauffeur is making a check of the newly introduced pneumatic tyres on his employer's motorcar. These would have absorbed the vibrations from the road a little better then the solid rubber ones on the spoked wheels of the open topped car parked behind. Visible are the coach springs of this car's suspension, which owe their origin to vehicles like the cart seen progressing up Verulam Road towards the Red Lion. Maybe the lady with the coach built pram to the left of the picture is the nanny to one of the many wealthy families who lived in St Albans in 1921. As she looks back she may recognise the chauffeur or the top hatted groom, or maybe she knows the gentleman walking towards Younger's shop. He is wearing the fashionable straw boater. The manufacture of hats was an important industry in St

Albans up to the first world war. It had begun as a women's home industry in the cottages around St Albans. The chalk soil of Hertfordshire produced long stemmed wheat that was pliable and suitable for plaiting. They would plait ten-inch lengths of straw together to form a 'score', a twenty-yard length of plait. This would then be taken to St Albans Plait Market, near the Clock Tower, or later to the Corn Exchange, where they would receive payment and the next supply of straw. Eventually factories were established and cheaper Japanese plait made from rice straw became more fashionable, because it made lighter, thus bringing about the end of this cottage industry. Boaters, as the hats were called, were made by firms such as Dunham and Martin for Eton, Rugby, Harrow and several more schools. They were shipped to America and other parts of the world.

There is a mystery as to why the Clock Tower, built between 1403 and 1412, was ever built at all. One theory is that it was a symbol of the town's independence. This medieval belfry is almost unique in England. It houses the great curfew bell 'Gabriel', which is older than the Tower itself dating from 1335. The only other structure like it is at Morpeth, Northumberland. It may seem strange that it could play some small part in the war at sea with Napoleon, but it did. Between 1807 and 1814 it had a telegraph apparatus on the roof. It was one stage in the rapid transmission of visual Admiralty signals between London and Yarmouth. It was once the centre of most trade and activity in the city with markets developing around it. It is rarely so quiet as here in 1925, and it would be rarer still to park a car as this one has been parked. The sign on the wall is not warning the driver that his car is at risk of being clamped, but is providing visitors with the interesting information that, close to this site, there once stood the 'Eleanor Cross'. This marked the spot where the body of Queen Eleanor, the wife of Edward 1, rested one night on its way to Westminster 13 December 1290.

Here on calm summer days the city guides gather their audience before commencing their tour of the historic city. There seems to be little need to warn them about their unruly behaviour, but there is a latrine, facing onto French Row, warning everyone to 'Commit no nuisance'. There is no mention of the penalty for doing so, but this warning has always brought a gentle smile to passing visitors. Motorcars were rapidly becoming more numerous, and the days of horse drawn transport were coming to an end. In Piccadilly, in 1926, the London police were experimenting with a traffic light system. A traffic policeman, referred to as a 'general', operated the lights while sitting in a box overlooking the area. The lights changed from red to white and then green. The Daily Mail reported that the drivers had rushed across when the lights changed, but the signals were intended for the police and not the drivers! These were the days of motoring. Five years after this picture was taken an Austin Seven coach built saloon cost one hundred and thirty pounds, and the tourer or the two-seater version cost one hundred and twenty two pounds and ten shillings each.

St. Albans Central Library

Left: Standing at the junction of the High Street and the Market Place is the fountain designed by Sir Gilbert Scott. He was working on the restoration of the Tower as well as producing a report on the crumbling Abbey, when he was commissioned to design the fountain. The Clock Tower can be see in the background, the ground floor of which was leased to the saddle maker. The fountain was commissioned by Mrs Isabella Worley, a rich widow, who came under great pressure from the council to place the fountain in St Peter's Street. She, however, was adamant that that it should be placed in the High Street, as in the picture. Mrs Worley thought that, placed by the Tower, it would be of greater benefit to the poor people. The focus of the city's activities now seem to be moving to St Peter's Street away from the High Street.

When the volume of traffic increased and the fountain caused some obstruction, it had to be removed from this spot. The fountain mysteriously disappeared! It had not drifted into the damp mist of night, like the vehicle in the photograph. It had divided itself into two parts. The bottom half into the garden of a house in St Peter's Street, and the top half into the garden of another house owned in London Road by Lord Brocket. Lord Brocket later bought the house in St Peter's Street. The Thrale family opened a restaurant and displayed the fountain as a decorative feature. In 1964 they gave it back to the council. The council obtained the top half from the new owner of the house in London Road and the two halves are now reunited in Victoria Square St Albans.

Above: Everyone, whatever their age, has a story to tell about owning, knowing someone who has owned, or driven in, or ridden in a car like those on show here. 'It went forever on a single cup full of petrol', they will say. They will tell how it broke down three times on the way home, but it eventually got them there. These were surely the golden days of motoring. These vehicles would even run, it seems, with monstrous solid public address systems welded firmly to their roofs. In the war years the public announcements could well have been issuing essential information in case of air raids. Many water tanks were placed at strategic points around the city, for fear of incendiary bombs. Maddock's shop had been selling poultry and game, but the premises are to let. With a good clean out, to get rid of that fishy smell, but with very little change to the outward appearance of the shop, the fashionable 'Next' clothes shop now occupies these premises. Many buildings in St Peter's Street have been demolished to make way for Marks and Spencer's, Woolworth's, Sainsbury's and other stores. Many of the fine Georgian houses, which once lined St Peter's Street, have had to be sacrificed to make way for the new. Above the trees at the end of the street we can see the tower of St Peter's Church. The building restoration was completed in 1908. The transepts had been demolished in 1802 as they were unsafe, and the tower had been cement rendered in an attempt to protect it. In front of the church is the attractive Green, on which stands the war memorial and gardens.

St Albans Central Library

Above: In its heyday, St Peter's Street was described as the most beautiful main street in Europe. The avenue of trees still gives elegance, and refinement to the Street, despite their lack of foliage. A Mr Gotto presented the trees to the city in 1881. At that time mansions for the very wealthy lined the street, many of them built in fine red brick. There are a few surviving to give those people waiting on the pavement an impression of how it must have been. The Post Office further up the road on the opposite side is a fine example. It is hard to believe that St Peter's Street has not always been St Alban's principal street. By the 1930s privately operated buses regularly ran from here, but for these folk there is not a single vehicle moving. Was this the time when the well known phrase 'there is never a bus when you want one' was coined? The pedestrian casually strolling across would have to take more care with today's volume of traffic. There are now pedestrian crossings, which take away the feeling of openness evident here in this picture. At the head of the street, in the mist can be seen the Town Hall, designed by George Smith in 1829. It came under threat when it was suggested, at the time when the new Civic Centre was planned, that it be taken from the Schedule of Listed Buildings, so that a supermarket could be built in its place. There was such an outcry from the people that the idea was quickly abandoned. In the end it was agreed that the land be given to the county for the building of the Civic Centre Complex, and the city bought the hall for a relatively small sum. Thank goodness that the

beauty of the street was not marred which it surely would have been if the area was punctuated by a supermarket rather than this Hall with its elegant facade.

Right: What a fine view of the wishbone shape made by The Market Place and French Row, linking with Chequer Street to join St Peter's Street. St Peter's Church, standing proudly at the head. After its extensive renovations of 1894-5, it could easily be thought to be a cathedral by any visitor to the city. In front of the church is the war memorial in St Peter's Green. The avenue of trees, which are a well known feature, point the way down to the Old Town Hall and Court House, which now houses the Tourist Information Office. To the right of St Peter's Street and Chequer Street there has been much redevelopment in recent years. The Civic buildings and the Maltings shopping complex now cover much of this land. That popular meeting place, the Clock Tower stands prominently at the junction with the High Street. The Waxhouse gate leading to the Abbey is visible at the bottom centre, but the Abbey is just below our line of view. Maybe the photographer was flying over in a Mosquito aeroplane to take this picture, after all they were developed a short distance away at Hatfield by the Sir Geoffrey De Havilland, or maybe one of the famous 'Halifax' bombers, made at the Handley Page factory at Radley. If we are to really let our imaginations take flight we could almost picture him hanging from an army surplus barrage balloon. However he managed to obtain this camera shot, it is an excellent picture of this beautiful city.

ooking down from the tower of St Michael's church, the road crosses the St Michael's Bridge over the river Ver. It is the oldest bridge in Hertfordshire still in use (built about 1765). The roof of the school can be seen beneath us. Hidden behind the tall pine, is the Six Bells pub. It has led a very confused life. In 1543 it was called Bell Croft, then in 1595 it became known as Le Bell in St

Michael's. In 1739 five bells were placed alongside the one bell at the church and the pub changed its name to the Six Bells. In early years the local people simplified matters and gave it the nickname the Ringers. Before the road climbs the hill, it passes Kingsbury Mill, busy grinding corn. The Mill has been carefully preserved as a museum, outlining the history of the mill and the area. Further along the road before it turns gently into

Fishpool Street, is the Kingsbury Manor House. To the right, hidden by the trees, stands the Blue Anchor Inn. Over the years it has been much altered but there are still some fine plaster ceilings. It must have been a welcome stopping off point for the men delivering the corn to the mill for grinding. Opposite the Blue Anchor is The Black Lion. Fishpool Street is a most attractive street with raised blue brick pavements, most necessary in the days when road surfaces would be at best cobbled and at their worst unmetalled. They soon became muddy in bad weather, and in the summer they would have to be sprayed to keep down the dust. In the foreground, to the right edge of the picture, is the Verulamium museum, founded shortly after the extensive excavations of Verulamium had been completed in the early 1930s.

St Albans Central Library

Left: Above the shops the towers of the Abbey, although in more formal circumstances properly known as the Cathedral and Abbey Church of St Albans, can be clearly seen from this high vantage point. To the people strolling in the streets below it must seem to have been there forever. A symbol of unshakeable faith. However, far from being unshakeable, in 1870 a clerk of works called John Chapple heard noises coming from the tower. On examination it was declared to be in a state of collapse. The assistance of architect Gilbert Scott was sought and he shored up the walls to prevent further movement. The one hundred and forty four foot tower was built with bricks taken from Roman buildings in Verulamium in the valley below the Abbey. It is one of the heaviest in the kingdom. There followed several years of work before the Abbey was safe once more. As the work was done new designs replaced the original gothic walls. The controversial Baron Grimthorpe, who was responsible for the restoration in 1880, is reputed to have described the perpendicular gothic as, 'thoroughly good for nothing'.

Above: The public library building in Victoria Street has changed little in outward appearance over the years. It is a fine building with an ornamental carved lintel above the door. The mayor Dr Eustace H Lipscombe laid its foundation stone in 1910. It can be seen on the left hand pillar of the doorway. It replaced the old library, which had seen good use, but was unable to cope with the increase in demand. The old library stood at the opposite side of the road, where the Maltings Shopping Complex now stands. The railings, seen here, survived the wartime government campaign to gather the raw materials needed for the war effort. Approximately forty two thousand tons of gates and railings were gathered for scrap by the Ministry Works Department. Aluminium pots and pans were collected door to door by groups organised by the Women's Voluntary Service. How useful this scrap was is debateable, but it gave everyone a sense of 'doing their bit'. The slogan 'Every scrap shortens the scrap' was the government propaganda. It was The Scottish philanthropist Andrew Carnegie who came to the aid of the council, when they planned this new library. Quite what they would have thought about it eventually becoming a public house can only be guessed at. Perhaps they would have been grateful that it has been named 'The Philanthropist and Firkin'. At least the generosity and benevolence of Andrew Carnegie continues to be recognised. Not only has the library not changed much, but also neither has the bus stop. It is still in the same place. And when the bus finally arrives, the two ladies with the comfortable prams will find that they are too big to fit in the luggage space. The felt hats could have been made in St Albans. The headscarf was practical wear during and after the war.

The Crystal Palace Public House, on the right of the picture, is now gone and replaced by a building that houses Gilberts Chartered Accountants. Across the road is the 'The Farmers Boy'. It is a tiny Inn, wedged between two shops, and has changed little over the years. At the top of the picture is the Ford garage where, above the showroom, was the dance hall where many gathered on a Saturday night. There was also another dance hall in Victoria Street where dances were held three times per week, on Tuesdays, Thursdays and Saturdays, Waterend Barn and the Ballito factory. The phenomenally successful Mini is passing its larger brother. The Maxi. When Austin and Morris joined forces to become British Leyland, they soon found themselves challenged by foreign imports. Whilst the Mini enjoyed popularity as a 'social symbol', and as a rally machine, the Maxi struggled in comparison. It had many of the innovative features of the Mini. The transverse engine made this a spacious car. It was aimed at a different, more conservative group within the market, who were offered much more choice. To go for a drive on Sunday was a pleasant release from the pressures of the week, and the cushions and backrests were almost essential in the car. Seat belts were optional. The shortage of raw materials after the war years was in the past. There was a settled optimism, as everyone enjoyed a new freedom. Young boys, with funny hair cuts from Liverpool, were besieged by screaming, hysterical girls, as their music was heard all over the world. It seemed that anything was possible, even our own painting and decorating, and other jobs around the house. The phrase 'Do It Yourself' was born.

Left: There is little wonder that the 77 foot tall Clock Tower has become a favourite meeting place, as it invites everyone to contemplate all the historic events that have taken place here over the years. Once there was a fountain, there has also been a market cross, even earlier a cross to commemorate the passing of the cortege of Eleanor, the beloved wife of Edward I. The Tower stands as a defiant statement of the people against the power of the Abbey. Restored in 1866 by Sir Gilbert Scott, it is built of similar materials to the tower of the Abbey, using some bricks taken from the Roman site of Verulamium. The ground floor of the Tower was designed to be leased as a shop. In 1915 C Pearce, a saddle and harness maker occupied it. What can be seen, as Halford's was also once owned by C Pearce, but as a fruiterer and fishmonger. This had once been the site of the Rose and Crown Inn. In the background we can see the Fleur De Lys Inn, where, by tradition, King John of France was held hostage for a time after his capture in the battle of Poitiers in 1356.

Below: The Mini car and the lady with the 'proper' pram, as many who remember these comfortable but impractical baby conveyances will call them, are entering High Street from Verulam Road. Ahead and to the left is George Street, which was once the main road into the town from the northwest before Verulam Road was cut in 1825. It was also one of the city's principal shopping streets, along with the High Street, before the rise of St Peter's Street between the wars. George Street got its name from the medieval George Inn. The large building,

standing on the corner of what is often known as 'Mayles corner', housed the City of London Flour and Grain Company in the 1880s. Now it is called 'The Tudor Tavern and Restaurant'. Next door is the cycle and motorcycle shop selling Rudge and Triumph motorcycles, as well as Humber motorcars and solid Raliegh cycles. All these products, which we believed at the time to be practical, reliable and everlasting, have ceased production and achieved the status of historic 'classics'. The shop now sells modern wrought iron furniture. No one in the sixties could have foreseen the amazing success of the revolutionary Mini. The design won the car many rally successes. The Mini became a film star and partook of a famous chase through Rome with the Mafia in hot pursuit. It became almost a fashion accessory. Many were decorated with wicker pattern doors, with 'go faster stripes', or had Union Jacks painted on the roof. Who can forget the car with the Union Jack, which appeared in the television series 'Butterflies'? Some vehicles became extinct because the Mini overshadowed them. The little brightly coloured bubble cars, the Isetta, the Messerschmitt, the Heinkel, fell victim to it. The orange plastic bodied Bond Bug tried to compete by appealing to the younger motorists. Other three wheelers such as the uncomfortable Bond Mini car, with one wheel leading, and the Berkeley with its revolutionary, and sleek shaped glass fibre body, all but lost favour as the Mini grew in popularity. To the right of the picture is the Red Lion, which, like its neighbour The Fleur De Lys, lost some of the yards at the rear as the road was cut through.

St Albans Central Library

The Boot Inn in market place stands on the corner of Boot Alley, opposite the Clock Tower. Originally the pub was a group of late medieval shops, but its origins as a pub are from the 1700s. Imagine the discomfort for the occupants and their guests when the bell 'Gabriel' rang the curfew at 4am and between 8pm and 9pm for a quarter of an hour. The bell last sounded for the funeral of Queen Victoria. Boot Alley leads through a cluster of buildings between Market Place and Chequer Street. In this area, and that which backs onto French Row, were many workshops making, amongst other things, shoes. French Row has had different names through the ages, one of which was 'Cordwainers' Row. A 'cordwainer' being a maker of shoes. This picture, looking so peaceful and quiet,

holds no clues as to how the atmosphere changes on market days. The street fills with stalls and the cries of market traders have rung through the street for hundreds of years. Fruit and vegetable stallholders seem to favour this corner by the Boot Inn. Below the pub sign there stands a red telephone box. The telephone company must have been surprised at the reaction from certain members of the public when they began the change from these cast iron boxes. Time had endeared them to the public, whose eyes could not accept the new. The ones that were removed from streets throughout the country were, surprisingly, bought by enthusiasts to decorate their gardens. They had achieved status of 'antiques' or 'collectables', reminding the people of a childhood that they were reluctant to release.

The scene is viewed from the railway bridge in Victoria Road with our backs to the Jail, which was built in 1867. As we face up the road towards the town, the view is dominated by the Trinity Church, standing, as it does, on the corner of Beaconsfield Road. Opposite the church a car attempts to cross from Alma Road. The bus is making its way to the Mile House Estate and will soon be passing an 'E-type' Jaguar, parked at the extreme right of our picture. Its sleek lines singled this out, as one of the true classic cars, even in the 1960s, and for that time its performance was surprising. The Jaguar's long sleek bonnet stretches out forever in front of the driver. The story was told of a young man who asked the salesman if they were nice to drive, to which he received the answer, 'Sir, you do not drive them, you aim them', sums up the publicity which they received. There have been very few changes, on the surface, at this end of Victoria Street. It was though, in times past, the street beyond the church was lined with trees. On the corner of Alma Road stood The Midland Railway Hotel. It would not have been built on this spot if the council of the time had allowed the intended railway to be brought to Romeland, or to St Michaels. The railway came to St Albans in 1858, but then it was only a branch line from Watford to the station at the foot of Holywell Hill. When the Midland Railway eventually arrived many of the coaching houses on Holywell Hill went out of business. At the top of the road, before it meets with Chequer Street, there have been developments on both sides of the road. Careful control has been applied so that the character of the city is preserved.

At the top of Holywell Hill, as the sign tells us, is the busy crossroads where the A6 and the A5 converge. It was hoped that the opening of the M1 would help to alleviate the problems at this junction, but if it did the difference was too small to be noticed.

This road has always been busy as it is part of the London to Holyhead Road. It was the first important stopping place for the coaches, and for this reason there were many Inns lining the road. The black and white timbered White Hart Inn is typical of the many, which there once was down this road. The entrance for coaches is now a car park entrance. The Inn was restored in the 1930s. On the junction, opposite the Peahen Inn, was the Peter Keys or the Cross Keys, long since demolished. Further down the hill were many more Coaching Houses, which have since disappeared, such as the Bull Inn, where Queen Elizabeth I stayed on one of her visits to the city. The sign on the White Hart directs visitors to the cathedral via Sumpters Yard. This yard is the place where packhorses, delivering to the Abbey, would be unloaded after their journey from London. The next building down the road, but sadly out of our picture, is a building with carved reliefs on the wall. It was owned by Samuel Ryder, who had a seed firm there. Famous though his packet seeds are, he is better known for his having donated the trophy that bears his name, 'The Ryder Cup'.

CAR PARK

HOTEL
AA

PRIVATE ROAD 5 CHILDREN AT PLAY

BEDFORD

4429 NK

Below: Many of the buildings in this picture have gone now. It is rumoured that the room above the garage once contained an excellent sprung dance floor. In the fifties and sixties, young people loved to go dancing. Regular dances were held at the Victoria Hall, Waterend Barn, or the Ballito factory. Many a person has glided across it to the strains of a quick step played by Joe Loss and his orchestra, a romantic tune from Victor Sylvester, or danced a slow foxtrot to the songs of Nat King Cole. Many will have danced to the waltz tune, 'Edelweiss', from the film 'The Sound of Music'. No doubt many more orchestras, singers and musicians will spring to mind. Eddie Calvert played his golden trumpet for our delight, and it was all 'Cherry Pink and Apple Blossom White' in those days. There was a clash now as Rock and Roll entered our vocabulary. In the late 50s and early 60s the more genteel dances had to step back whilst the 'Boppers' gyrated, swinging their partners around and even throwing them in the air. Little Richard stood and hit the piano keys and everybody seemed to go wild. The Italian suited 'Mods' put on their duffle coats and rode on their Lambretta and Vespa scooters to Brighton in order to fight with the 'Rockers'. The conservative adults were shocked as they witnessed this war that made little sense to them. The violent films such as 'The Blackboard Jungle' were blamed for this unruly behaviour. The 'thirties' style architecture and 'art deco' are now becoming fashionable again and, such buildings as this garage with its geometric frontage and clock, will be mourned by future generations. The site now has a modern red brick building, which will, we suppose, with time gain fashionable and historic status. Not a Japanese car anywhere to be seen, but the building with the rectangular gable end, at the brow of the hill at the far left of the picture, now sells Hyundai cars. Should any of the cars, seen here in this picture, drive along the London Road today, heads would turn and memories of the 'golden age' of motoring would be aroused.

Right: Once, above the battlements of the Abbey, there was a sharp pointed spire of the kind often known as 'Hertfordshire Spikes'. The spike was removed in 1833. Pilgrims took the short cut through the Waxhouse archway to the Abbey; this right of way has been carefully protected. The archway, next to Blundell's, is all that now remains of the factory run by the monks to produce candles and tapers for sale to the pilgrims. The premises occupied by Pearl Wallpaper and Lawley's was, in 1925, the impressive premises of Steabben and Son. On busy market days this area fills with stalls giving even the largest shops some serious competition. In earlier days vendors would lay their wares on the ground in wicker baskets, metal wheeled hand carts and various horse drawn vehicles would noisily go about their business in this area as they have done since Saxon times. Over the years it has grown and now stretches from here to St. Peter's Street on market days.

The driver of the Sunbeam Rapier, which is disappearing around the corner, may not be aware that he has passed, what was at one time one of the city's most important buildings the 'Moot Hall', now W H Smith occupy the ground floor premises. Sometimes referred to as the 'Old Town Hall', it has been occupied before by booksellers and stationers. Gibbs and Bamforth traded here in the late 1800s and early 1900s. To rear of the premises, down Dagnall Street they had their printing works and were the proprietors of the St Albans and Herts Advertiser. In those days the beams were not exposed as they are in this picture. It continued as the meeting place for the council

until the Town Hall, seen on the very left of the picture, opened in 1831. It was built on a design by George Smith. It functioned as a combined Court House and Town Hall. The corporation sold the Moot Hall. The building, which stands at the head of the road, is known as 'the Gables'. Laura Ashley shops now occupy it. In the late 1800s Worsell the

Drapers vacated the premises and it came under threat of demolition. Public pressure saved this historic building. True to form, the people preserved their historic heritage for posterity.

This area comes to life with the cries of street vendors every Saturday and Wednesday, as it has done for hundreds of years.

St Albans Central Library

St Albans Central Library

At leisure

L ocal tradition suggests that the very picturesque French Row, was renamed because French prisoners, including King John of France, captured at the battle of Poitiers were billeted here. Previously it had been called Cobblers Row or Cordwainers Row, aptly named since shoemakers occupied many of the shops in this area. The man posing nonchalantly against the wall, would, in a short time after the photograph was taken, have been eligible for the armed forces. The Union Jacks flying from the window of the 'Christopher Inn',

echo the feelings of national pride of the times between the two wars. The Christopher has not been an inn since about 1875, and was a lodging house up to the end of the second world war. Around 1910, rooms in the Christopher were occupied by the 'Clock Tower Toilet Club', the function of this group is not certain and it may be wise to simply let the matter rest. Traffic must have been giving the members of the City Council sufficient concern for them to erect the 'No Entry' sign at the end of French Row. By 1976 the street was pedestrianised.

'The Fighting Cocks' or 'Ye Old Fighting Cocks' boasts proudly from the notice on the wall that it is the oldest inhabited public house in the country. Some historians say that its hexagonal structure is derived from a pigeon house moved here in the sixteenth century from the grounds of the dissolved Abbey. Others suggest that it may have been a monks' fishing lodge. Along the banks of the River Ver, and around the lake in the park, there are pleasant walks. The ducks, geese and swans expect all walkers to have some tasty titbits for them, and come to greet people in the park. For the people enjoying locally brewed ale and basking in the sunshine, it is simply the perfect spot to meet friends returning from the shops or resting after a walk. This tranquil scene is in contrast with the days when bets were shouted as men proudly held fighting cockerels high. Then, often with

sharp spurs attached to their heels, the birds were placed in the pit to viciously attack as we can see graphically depicted on the sign above the path. The Inn was renamed 'The Fisherman' when the sport became illegal in 1849. The Inn is reputed to have once provided accommodation for Oliver Cromwell for a night, during the civil war. A notice outside tells the visitor that there are underground tunnels beneath the Inn, which provide useful bolt holes in troubled times. Legend tells of rich treasures hidden by monks somewhere in the network of passages that supposedly run under the ground in this area. One story is told of a man who was lost in the tunnels but could hear the sound of people singing. He shouted, and the frightened people in the Abbey Church could hear his cries coming from within the hollow pillar in the church. When they had overcome their fear it is said that they released him.

The children's' library is now the main bar of the 'Philanthropist and Firkin' public house. Many of us will still feel that rush of excitement when they notice the Meccano magazine on the rack beneath the window. It seemed possible to build anything with Meccano. Many a builder or engineer must have gained their interest in their chosen career as a result of reading this publication. On the shelf above are 'The Scout' and 'Aero Modeller'. How appropriate for a city which raised money for the building of a spitfire. The City of St Albans P8144 went into service in 1941 with the 41st Squadron. About this time the 'Eagle' comic was born. Many a boy had to wait until his father had finished reading it before he could find out if Dan Dare, space pilot, had escaped the clutches of the Mekon. In the corner the girls are gathered around, what was probably thought to be more appropriate literature for them than the 'Hotspur', or 'The Wizard', or books about the Air Ace 'Biggles', which were far too violent for the gentler sex. 'Fairy stories', and 'Story Books' are a more suitable diet. 'Sexist' was not a word that had yet been invented and the librarian at the desk would have been comfortable with this clear statement of their position in life. The children's newspaper could well be announcing the end of rationing in 1954. How many remember the joy of not being limited to two ounces of sweets. Even though rationing ceased it was not always possible to buy whatever was wanted for shortages in some things became even more severe for a time. It is noticeable how the girls wore headscarves similar to those their mothers would wear. The boys hair, carefully parted and held in place with a little 'Brylcream' no doubt, is displaying the well known 'short back and sides' style, which is trimmed well clear of the ears. Through the window The School of Science and Art can be seen. It was built before the library. The roundels decorating the walls are portraits of Davy, Bacon and Hogarth, representing science, art, and literature.

Above: The big top is erected, and daily performances are boldly advertised at either side of the door. The pitch is probably in Verulamium Park. The mobile ticket box is ready to receive the crowds, though it seems remarkably quiet. Only the Ringmaster is there to pose for the photographer in this early picture taken at the time when Bertram Mills started his tenting circus in the early 1930s. The story is told that Bertram Mills, who owned a carriage building company, went to a circus performance at Olympia in 1919 presented by Wilkens and Young. When asked what he thought of the show he replied that if he could not do better himself he would eat his hat. He must have been taken up on the boast, because he gave the Christmas Circus at Olympia from 1920 to 1966. He began his tenting circus after the famous Barnum and Bailey Circus had come to England, and copied their idea of entertaining many of London's high society to a party every time he was to launch special events, or new acts, at the circus. He travelled throughout Europe searching for speciality acts for his show. Many will remember the excitement as the large globe lights shone, powered by the noisy generators, and people formed orderly queues to shuffle their way into the tent. There they would sit on stepped benches waiting for the band to strike up the music. Ice cream and toffee apples were always on sale. The toffee on the apples was dark brown and formed a flat top where the apple had stood while the toffee hardened. The stick never seemed to stay in the sour apple. For many children the stars, whatever the billing said, were the clowns. Bertram Mills had three very popular clowns called Coco, Percy Huxter, and Little Billy. They threw water at one another, and attacked each other, and anyone near, with custard pies. They tormented the Ringmaster as he organised and presented the acts. The Ringmaster looked magnificent in his hunting kit, a scarlet tailcoat, a top hat, white buckskin breeches and black riding boots, which were introduced, or maybe revived, by Bertram Mills Circus in 1921. He cracked his whip to show that he was in charge, and introduced the performers who were always 'the greatest'. We were told how privileged we were to be entertained by those who had performed for the Kings, Queens and Nobility of Europe.

The Odeon cinema is now closed and searching for a new purpose. The Art Deco style architecture stands like a deserving monument to the history of the cinema, which, it can be argued had its origins here. Arthur Melbourne-Cooper was born at a house in the London Road. His father was a photographer and Arthur followed in his footsteps. As soon as he was old enough he joined the family business. He became friends with a man called Birt Acres who had similar interests and they experimented with 'moving pictures'. They made a number of films including what must be one of the first news films showing the Prince of Wales opening the Manchester Ship Canal. In 1903 he took pictures of the Grand National at half past three, developed his film in the toilet on the train coming home and showed it at the Empire Leicester Square in the evening. That must have shaken the audience who were still trying to grasp the magical idea of moving pictures. He then decided to open his own cinema. He set up in the old 'Poly' in London Road

where the Odeon now stands. It was a big hall and dances and concerts were held during the week, and 'Poly Pops' on Saturdays. The old Poly was burnt down, but Arthur saw a positive side to this accident. He decided to build a cinema to his own design. He built the St Albans Picture Palace. He introduced some ideas which the public found strange at first, but it set the pattern for all cinemas for a long time into the future. There were tip-up seats. Two performances of moving pictures were given every night. Charges of 2d, 4d, and 6d were made but many thought they were being cheated when the most expensive seats were at the back. Soon they realised that this was the best place to be. It is said that, on the opening night, people had to be turned away because the house was full. This design became the pattern for all cinemas, what would we have missed if children had not been allowed to sit on the first two rows for mere coppers? Everybody remembers the usherette who kept them in order; she was more frightening than the threat of an invasion.

Events & occasions

There is no reason to believe that the bow under the gentleman's chin rotates when the power is switched on, but we do think that there is a comic element to this probably serious experiment. The audience is engrossed in the lines produced on the graph by the impulses from the man's brain, and not a single smile from any of them. The man seems comfortable on the well cushioned settee and appears to be in no danger. During the war Marconi shared part of Ballito's premises and made radar equipment and components. Many companies in St Albans were involved in secret work for the government. The 'pinging sound' heard in any submarine film, usually at the height of tension as the German U-boat approaches, comes from an underwater sound ranging system. These were often referred to as ASDIC and many were made at a factory in Beaconsfield Road, St Albans. The young man in the centre, wearing short trousers, seems to have missed an important milestone in his life. In the 1940s and 1950s boys were persuaded into believing a theory that it was healthy, up to the age of thirteen or so, to wear short trousers and allow air to circulate around their legs. Schools wrote it into their school uniform policies that boys should be persuaded not to get into long trousers too early in life. For a boy to receive his first pair of long pants was the equivalent of any 'coming of age ' ceremony anywhere in the world. With each leg of the trousers came the recognition that they were now adult and able to accept responsibility.

Dinah Sheridan and her husband are seen here arriving at the Gaumont Cinema in Stanhope Road for the Premiere of the film 'Genevieve'. Dinah Sheridan was born not very far away in Welwyn Garden City. The film was a huge success she and her film partner, played by John Gregson, raced the vintage car 'Genevieve' to London Bridge. A fellow vintage car enthusiast played by Kenneth More had challenged them. The lovely Kay Kendal was Kenneth More's passenger on this race to the capital. It was a beautiful story with a happy ending, even if 'Genevieve' did not win the race.

In 1953 the country was still recovering from the effects of the war, and rationing continued for a further year. People still needed the boost to their morale. They needed the escape from everyday life that such a film, with a pleasant story and theme tune, could provide. It was full of beautiful people. Even the opposition in the race, despite their unsportsmanlike behaviour, turned out good in the end. And with that the audience all left the cinema smiling, humming and whistling and the world did not seem a bad place after all. Fish and chips on the way home were not too expensive either.

In the 1930s the Earl of Verulam decided to sell a large part of his estate. Some of it covered the site of the Roman town of Verulamium, which the council decided to buy to create a park for the people of St Albans. Before that happened, the Archaeological Society of Great Britain decided to raise a team to make as thorough an excavation as possible. They appointed Dr Mortimer Wheeler and Mrs Tessa Wheeler to lead the party. The excavations lasted from 1930 to 1934, and they uncovered some amazing finds. They contributed so much to our knowledge of Roman Britain that it became necessary to build a museum to house the treasures. On the photograph we can see the opening ceremony on the 8 May 1939. Standing at the large Bakelite microphone, is the mayor.

Behind him at the table, is Princess Mary the younger sister of George VI. Also at the table, nervously clutching his notes in preparation for the opening ceremony, which he is about to perform, is the Earl of Harewood. The lady, with the fashionable elbow length gloves and straw hat, is the mayoress. When the excavations were completed, the land was levelled and a sports ground laid. The field outside the wall was hollowed out to form the beautiful lake we all enjoy today. During the war this lake was drained of water, because, on a moonlit night, it could be seen clearly by the enemy's bombers. The pilots used it as a point of navigation for a turn and second run on London. It was a mere gesture as they had a more prominent marker in the tower of the Abbey, which it was impossible to hide.

Both pages: In 1939 Britain's Prime Minister Neville Chamberlain had made his announcement to the waiting people of Britain that '...this country is at war with Germany.' The country rolled up its sleeves and prepared for the inevitable. This war would be different from other wars. This time planes had the ability to fly further and carry a heavier load, and air raids were fully expected. Air raid shelters were obviously going to be needed, and shelters were built on open places across towns and cities.

By the time war was declared an army of volunteers of both sexes had already been recruited to form an Air Raid Protection service. At first ARP personnel were unpaid volun-

teers but when war broke out in September 1939 they became paid staff. It was their job to patrol specified areas, making sure that no chinks of light broke the blackout restrictions, checking the safety of local residents, being alert for gas attacks, air raids and unexploded bombs. The exceptional work done by Air Raid Wardens in dealing with incendiaries, giving first aid to the injured, helping to rescue victims from their bombed-out properties, clearing away rubble, and a thousand and one other tasks became legendary; during the second world war nearly as many private citizens were killed as troops - and many of them were the gallant ARP wardens. At the beginning of the war Sir Anthony Eden, Secretary of State for War, appealed in a radio broadcast for men between

17 and 65 to make up a new force, the Local Defence Volunteers, to guard vulnerable points from possible Nazi attack. Within a very short time the first men were putting their names down. At first the new force had to improvise; there were no weapons to spare and men had to rely on sticks, shotguns handed in by local people, and on sheer determination . Weapons and uniforms did not become available for several months.

In July the Local Defence Volunteers was renamed the Home Guard, and by the following year were a force to be reckoned with. Television programmes such as 'Dad's Army' have unfortunately associated the Home Guard with comedy, but in fact they performed much important work. The Guard posted sentries to watch for possible aircraft or parachute landings at likely spots such as disused aerodromes, golf courses on the outskirts of towns, local parks and racecourses.

They manned anti-aircraft rocket guns, liaised with other units and with regular troops, set up communications and organised balloon barrages.

Other preparations were hastily made. Place names and other identifying marks were obliterated to confuse the enemy about exactly where they were. Notices went up everywhere giving good advice to citizens on a number of issues. 'Keep Mum - she's not so dumb' warned people to take care what kind of information they passed on, as the person they were speaking to could be an enemy.

Older readers will remember how difficult it was to find certain items in the shops during the war; combs, soap, cosmetics, hairgrips, elastic, buttons, zips - all were virtually impossible to buy as factories that once produced these items had been turned over to war work. Stockings were in short supply, and resourceful women resorted to colouring their legs with gravy browning or with a mixture of sand and water. Beetroot juice was found to be a good substitute for lipstick. Clothes rationing was introduced in 1941, and everyone had 66 coupons per year. Eleven coupons would buy a dress, and sixteen were needed for a coat. The number of coupons was later reduced to 40 per person. People were required to save material where they could - ladies' hemlines went up considerably, and skirts were not allowed to have lots of pleats. Some found clever ways around the regulations by using materials that were not rationed. Blackout material could be embroidered and made into blouses or skirts, and dyed sugar sacks were turned into curtains.

Below: The Queen Mother has always held a special place in the hearts of the people of St Albans. Here she is seen arriving in Verulamium Park as the young cadet hoists the flag. She came to join in the celebration of the one thousandth anniversary of the founding of the three churches, St Peter's, St Stephen's and St Michael's, by Abbott Ulsinus in 948AD. According to reports of the day there had been heavy rain during the afternoon threatening the performances, which were to take place in the evening. As the Queen Mother stepped out of the car the sun came out and a bright rainbow arched over the Abbey Tower. No producer could have asked for a more spectacular backcloth for any performance. Mr Cyril Swinson, who also acted as the pageant master, wrote the script. It was a most successful performance. The pageant held in 1907 had enacted the history of St Albans up to the visit of Queen Elizabeth I. This millenary pageant extended to include the constitution of St Albans as a city.

Among the other honoured guests, were the mayor and some councillors from the Danish town of Odense. Odense too is an Abbey town with the Abbey dedicated to St Alban. There is a story that Danes raided the Abbey, at St Albans. They stole the bones of the saint and took them back to Odense. They then dedicated their church to the saint. The monks of the Abbey at St Albans, however, secretly went to Odense and stole them back again. This fact the Danes deny, and claim that they still possess the bones. To add to the confusion the monks of Ely also claimed that they were the ones who had the bones of the saint!

Right: In 1961 St Albans corporation decided to invite Elizabeth the Queen Mother to become an honorary freeman. She did them the honour of accepting. She had always been close to the hearts of the people in the area, who felt that she was one of their own as she had been born in the county. It is surprising perhaps that no other town in the county had considered this action themselves. On 13th April of that year she came to the city. Her first stop was the Abbey, and, after lunch, to the town hall where she inspected a guard of honour from the Hertfordshire Regiment, of which she is colonel. She was then presented with the scroll of freedom by the Mayor, Elsie Toms, and signed the roll. The scroll, inscribed by a local artist, was presented inside a silver and crystal casket, designed and made by a local silversmith. Fine craftsmen have always gravitated towards this city and its Abbey. During the eighteenth century the freedom was bought and sold by corrupt officials. Consequently the custom was eyed with suspicion for a time and cities, like St Albans, were cautious about bestowing it on anyone. There were no such misgivings when it was bestowed upon the Queen Mother. The decision to do so was a popular one with the people who gathered to witness this historic event. She attracted as much support, with as many fans as the Beatles. Perhaps they were humming 'She loves you, yea, yea, yea'?

St Albans Central Library

The Union Jack is hoisted on the flagstaff, and the orderly crowd are waiting for a Royal visitor to arrive. It is probably 1961 when the Queen Mother visited the city to graciously accept their offer to make her Honorary Freeman of the City of St Albans. It looks as if it is a pleasant summer day, judging from the printed cotton dresses that are in evidence. It seems better weather than the occasion when she attended the Millenary pageant when the weather was reported showery. Whatever the occasion the crowd are disciplined and patient as they wait on the pavement. The gentlemen in the picture are wearing their suits, or after careful thought, a sports jacket. These are times when the correct attire for every occasion was very important. There were unwritten rules of dress, which must be observed. A man, in a profession or a job of work which necessitated him to meet the public in any official capacity, was expected to wear a white

collar and a tie. In the late 50s and early 60s there was a challenge to these conventions. Suddenly pastel coloured shirts came into vogue, and TV detectives shocked the public with their outrageous haircuts emulating pop stars. Jason King, who was a kind of frilly multicoloured James Bond, with long side burns, and cravats with flowers printed on them, shocked the conservatively dressed adult. Little wonder a song with the words, 'why can't they be like we were, perfect in every way?' reached

the charts. Many blamed it on the introduction of Rock and Roll music imported from America. The discipline and self-control demonstrated in this photograph disappeared when Bill Haley and the Comets flashed onto the cinema screen in the film 'Rock Around The Clock'. Cinema seats were torn to pieces, girls fainted, and young people rioted. In some towns the councils banned the film. The new sense of the freedom that had been fought for in the recent war was being fully explored.

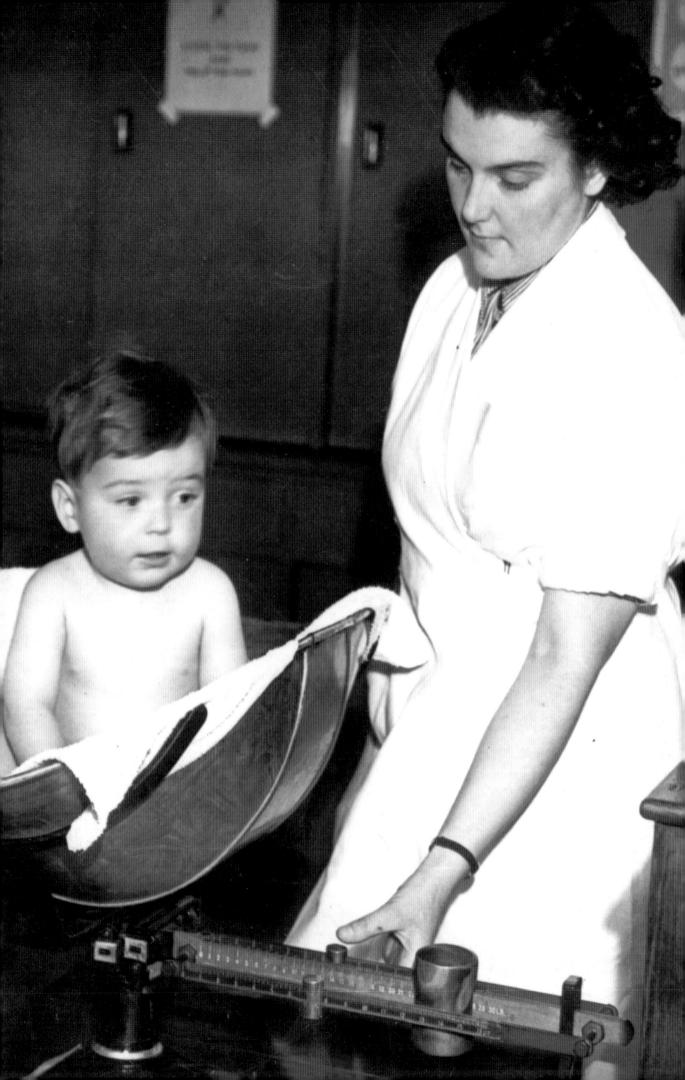

Both pages: It was possibly the acute wartime shortages of food and supplies which made doctors, health workers and mothers alike very aware of the health of the new generation, and children were carefully weighed, measured and immunised against the illnesses that had at one time meant disfigurement or even death *(facing page)*. A vaccine for polio, the scourge of former years which left behind its terrible mark of wasted and useless limbs, only came later, however. American scientist Jonas Edward Salk developed a vaccine in 1955, and an oral vaccine was produced in 1960. The vaccines brought the dreaded disease under control and today polio is rarely seen. On a day to day basis, vitamins were vital to the health of children, and long before the advent of the cod liver oil capsule, the recommended spoonful of cod liver oil was administered to the youngest children every day in schools and nurseries around the country during the 1940s. Children might have screwed up their noses at the fishy taste, but the nourishing cod liver oil went a long way towards keeping them healthy. The vitamin-packed orange juice was far more palatable, and artful mothers would often use the orange juice as a bribe: no cod liver oil, no orange juice. Following hard on the heels of the oil, the juice took away the distinctive taste that was disliked by so many children. Ante-natal clinics

did all they could to check on the diet, blood pressure and vitamin intake of mothers to be; our carefully posed photograph, taken in an ante-natal clinic in the 1930s, records at least the cleanliness and tidiness that was to their great credit *(bottom)*. And when the tiny new citizen finally arrived, there were health visitors to pay friendly calls on families in their homes to check on the health and happiness of mothers and babies *(left)*. National Dried Milk for babies was also made available to mothers, and before today's push towards natural feeding NDM was for decades very much in vogue. We need to remember that at the time of these photographs the National Health service did not exist, and in fact the NHS only came into operation after World War II in July 1948.

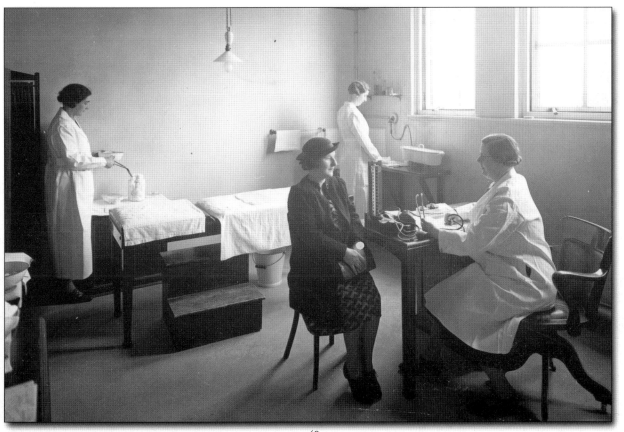

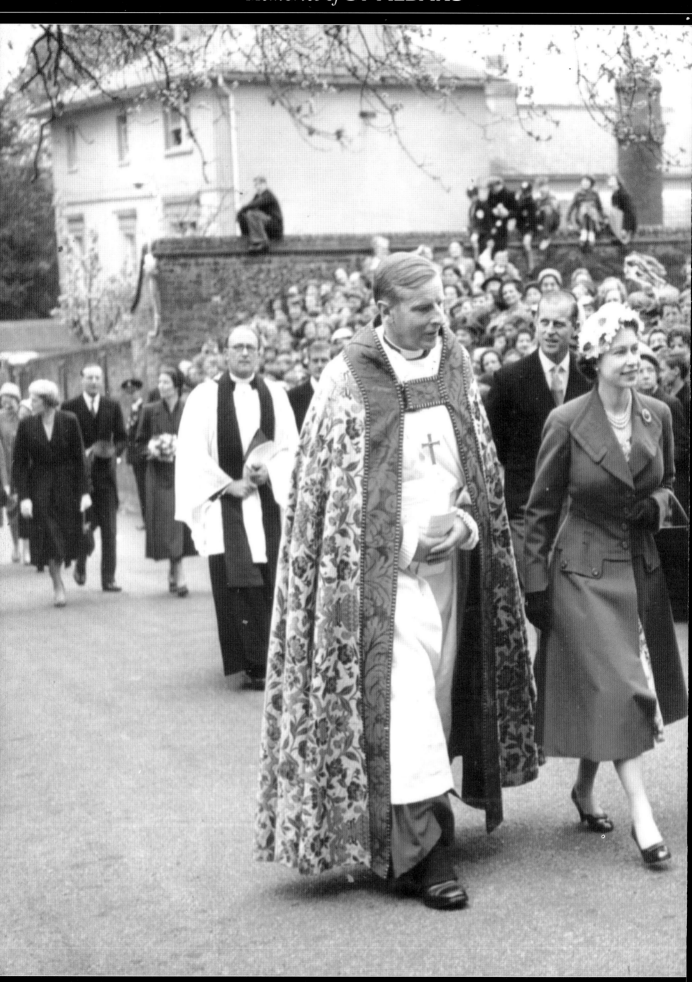

St Albans Central Library

The orderly crowd, waiting on the banked steps of George Henry Pownall Glossop's memorial garden, seem to be keeping an orderly line through their own self-discipline without great effort from the policewoman. Some have gained a better vantage point by standing on the walls of the Abbey Gate House. They all have an excellent view of the queen as she strolls up the hill towards the Abbey Gateway. She is chatting with the Right Reverend Edward Michael Gresford Jones as they make their way to the Abbey for the distribution of Maundy Money in 1957.

At the top of the lane they would have turned towards the Abbey, in front of the Gateway, from where the photographer must have taken this picture. The Gateway is all that remains to give a glimpse of the past magnificence of the monastery. This Gateway would once have been the point where such royal visitors, and their accompanying throng, would have been greeted. Outside this entrance to the monastery grounds is a rectangular space, which is still called Romeland, where the Abbott and officials would have welcomed the visitors. They would then have proceeded through the gate followed by their retinue.

From 1553 to 1869 the Gateway had had a less glamorous role as a prison. Since 1871 it formed a part of St Alban's School.

The queen smiles appreciatively at the young attendants in their smart apparel, as she leaves the Abbey having distributed the Royal Maundy Money to the same number of deserving ladies and gentlemen as her age. On Maundy Thursday, the Thursday before Easter, the sovereign gives out purses of money to the poor. In even numbered years this takes place at Westminster Abbey, and in odd numbered years, such as this in 1957, at others venues around the country. Today the queen gives each of the chosen recipients three leather purses. The men receive two white and one red purse, and the ladies are given a green, a white, and a red purse.

From as early as 600 AD monarchs have performed this ceremony though, as well as distributing the gifts, would have washed, dried and kissed the feet of a number of poor people as a sign of humility. Elizabeth the First would have given out quite a mixed hamper of money, an assortment of fish which would include a half salmon, cloth to make a garment, a wooden dish of red wine, as well as the apron and towel used in the ceremonial washing of the feet. All these gifts were put into a wicker basket called a 'maund' and given to the people. Both she and the Dean carry a posy of flowers. The Duke chats with Michael Gresford Jones, on whom the Freedom of the City was conferred in 1969.

On the move

S porting an array of different motorcycles, starting with the wing badged Matchless and a B S A motorcycle, the St Albans National Fire Service pose proudly for the camera. The rider third from the right seems far too young to be riding a motorcycle, let alone being a member of the service. All realised that, at times of war, everybody had to make a contribution. The headlamps were hooded because of the blackout regulations. The blackout began half an hour before sunset and ended half an hour after sunrise. In February 1940 summer time was brought forward and continued all year long to allow the people extra daylight in the evening. The most dangerous time to be on the roads at night was the first month of the war. The message had been taken very seriously that enemy aircraft could see even a faint light that many drove with no lights at all. Even though lamp-posts and kerb edges were painted with white or luminous paint there were many accidents. The headlight hoods, which can be seen on these motorcycles, allowed some light be deflected downwards. More people were killed in St Albans as a result of accidents attributable to the blackout than were killed by air raids. The blackout ended in 1944 when there were still some restrictions, but some light was allowed to show. The people had grown so accustomed to the blackout that they continued because they thought they could now see a possible end to the war.

Above: The wrought and cast iron pillars stand like trees supporting the roof of platform 1, are typical of many throughout Britain. Fringed by a wooden decorative border, it brings back fond memories of waiting beneath it for the noisy, powerful, steam train which would hiss as the brakes were applied. We would climb aboard carrying our brown leather suitcases. Maybe we were going to one of the many seaside resorts advertised on lithographed posters displayed on the walls of the waiting rooms. As we sat listening to the gasping and chugging of the train as it gathered momentum we could have been sucking one of the 'Glacier Mints' advertised on the enamelled tin poster on the right of the picture. Through the shine we can just see the polar bear precariously balanced on the clear mint. It could well have been that the children were not getting onto a train to go on holiday, but were arriving in St Albans due to the threat of air raids in the cities and coastal towns. St Albans had been designated a 'reception area'. During the first week of war the city received around six thousand evacuees. They were met at the station by members of the WVS (Women's Voluntary Service). They were then taken to distribution centres to be told where they would be living. Many would have worn labels, like pieces of luggage, bearing their names and other information about them. As the months went by and there were no air raids, many returned home. This period was called the 'Phoney War'. Many were re-evacuated in June 1940 as the attacks on London began.

Right: The roofs bristle with the more complicated television aerials, which could now bring three channels to our screens. There was now a new third channel with the catchy advert 'You're going well, you're going Shell'. Anyone who lived through the sixties will not want their attention bringing to the Shell sign above the garage for fear that they will have that famous television advertisement 'jingle' going through their minds and stick there for a long time. The reader may remember Georgie Fame, whose backing group was 'The Blue Flames', recorded the song 'Getaway', which was also used by Shell in another advert for their product. To the left is the Old London Road running into Sopwell Lane and into Holywell Hill. It is the most direct route to the Abbey. Packhorses and stagecoaches would have travelled this route, passing the gallows, which were erected on Sopwell Lane. On the site of this garage once stood the tollgate house. The gate extended across the New London Road, barring the way up into the town. It, along with 'The Firs', a house that stood next to it, was demolished about 1890. The St Albans Filling Station replaced them later. The Ford Garage has now been invaded by the French, and Renault cars are now sold on this very spot. Beyond the garage are the Priory Court flats. If this photograph was taken in 1958, we had better have a good look at the Morris Minor because Alfred Hinds had made his third escape from prison. This time he had escaped from Chelmsford prison in Essex making his getaway in a Morris Minor!

Bottom: Another of the gleaming fleet of lorries loading for the St Albans Cooperative Society Dairy Department. There would be little traffic to interfere with deliveries for this St Albans Cooperative Dairy lorry, except at the notorious Peahen crossroads where the two main roads intersect. Most people were only just beginning to realise that the motorcar was not too far beyond their reach. Before they had been only for the very wealthy. The age of the motorcar was here, and the roads of St Albans were about to feel the impact. But for the moment most people used public transport. As early as 1909 buses ran from the market square to Fleetville several times per day. Very soon another ran in the opposite direction to Dunstable. The London General Omnibus Company ran an open topped bus from St Albans to London. The St Albans Steam Carriage Company built a steam road machine with a body built with sufficient seats for fifty passengers. It was based on an idea that had been tried by an inventor called Richard Trevithick. They may have caused some trouble to the milkmen in those days delivering from their horse and trap. Customers would come from their homes with their jugs and other receptacles. The milkman filled from a churn via a pint, half pint, or gill measure.

Right: What a pleasant sight this well polished milk lorry must have been to those, who in the fifties still remembered clearly the dry 'Household' powdered milk that they had had to endure during the war. Rationing had started on 8 January 1940. Powdered egg was imported from America from June 1942, as fresh eggs were in short supply. Unless, that is, you knew someone who could trade on the black market. The 'Dig for Victory' campaign was

introduced in May 1939. Many turned their gardens over to food production, and every spare bit of land was utilised. Rationing continued for a few years after the war. Even building materials had to be controlled, as houses were in short supply. 'Necessity' invented the 'prefab'. The prefabrication of parts allowed for faster building erection. Many, who lived in the 'prefabs', claimed to love them because they were so compact, easy to keep warm, and very cosy. The same building techniques applied to other houses built at the end of the forties and the early fifties. It created an unmistakable 'utilities' look. They were built 'under licence' and often had prefabricated windows. Many of which were made from metal, which had a tendency to bend after some use so that they did not fit perfectly. Many were suspicious of this new fashion of 'pebble-dashing', as it was thought that it could hide inferior materials or inferior workmanship. To have a garage built onto the house was now most desirable. Petrol, the first commodity to be rationed, was slowly becoming more plentiful.

The sign advertising Players cigarettes would now be illegal, and, now that the building is occupied by the West Hertfordshire Community Health Care Unit, would be most inappropriate. At this time though such advertising was acceptable, and it was highly fashionable. Many of our heroes of the silver screen always seemed to have a cigarette hanging from their lips. It seemed almost essential for the tough guys, like Humphrey Bogart, to smoke incessantly. There is an interesting development in the evolution of the motorcar depicted in this picture. There is a contrast between the vehicle in the right foreground, which was built on a chassis, with the vehicles parked at the side of the road whose body shells were designed to have all other components bolted to them. The post office is still operating at the same place, although the old post boxes are now disappearing from our streets. Around the corner to the left, the old Beehive Public House still thrives. Below the Beehive pub is Keyfields Terrace. It owes its name to a time long ago when the men of the town gathered in the 'keyfields' to practice their archery skills so that they were prepared to defend the town should the need arise. At the time of this picture c1955, there would have been many men for whom that idea would seem familiar. 'The Home Guard' had been formed in 1940 as the Local Defence Volunteers (LDV). It was their duty to guard Britain in the event of an invasion by the Germans. They did not have uniforms when they were first formed, neither did they have weapons. Most of them were men who were too old to join the regular army, or had been rejected on medical grounds. Affectionately known as 'Dad's Army', and immortalised now by the popular television programme.

> *Keyfields Terrace owes its name to a time long ago when the men of the town gathered in the 'keyfields' to practice their archery skills*

The Peahen Hotel stands on the corner of what has always been an extremely dangerous road junction, where the A6 and A5 converge. This was once the busiest junction in Britain, and some even said in Europe. So many accidents occurred that something had to be done. At first police stood in the middle of the road every day directing the traffic. This must have proved expensive in terms of money and manpower. It was also not particularly efficient. Then a radical solution was found. Some of the first pad-operated traffic lights ever used were installed here to try to alleviate the problem. New words were added to our language, like the Czech word 'robot' to describe the lights. Drivers became skilled at running over the rubber pads which operated the lights at the right speed, or would craftily slip into reverse and give them another press in order to get them to change in their favour. Small boys played a game of standing on the pads to make the lights change, when there was no traffic about. This is the main London Road and, if we picture the traffic in it being substituted by stagecoaches, we would have an inkling of what it must have been like at the height of stagecoach days. It is thought that as many as seventy stagecoaches per day would come up this road, offering much interest, no doubt, to the people looking from the balcony or bay window of the Peahen Hotel. The Peahen Hotel started life as a coaching Inn and had extensive stable facilities. The entrance to which was from Chequer Street. In the yard of the Inn there is still a sign asking you to 'ring for the ostler'. Nobody ever does these days, as there seems to be no bell.

Not just any old iron

'**A**rrghh-an-oone'! When was the last time you heard the unmistakable cry of a rag and bone man down your road? Did it ever occur to you that the once familiar might one day soon never be heard again?

The rag and bone man was once part of our everyday world. The business was always about recycling old and unwanted goods to turn them into new ones.

One firm which has made the transition from the horse and cart days to become a huge business with impeccable green credentials is the St Albans company of Pearce Recycling. The company was founded in 1869 by Joshua Pearce who had moved to the area in 1860. Joshua took the Sugar Loaf pub near to where the Tudor Tavern stands. He soon became interested in scrap metal - no doubt because the Sugar Loaf was a regular meeting place for local scrap

Above: Paperwork from 1874. Below: Pearce's shop pictured in the early 1900s.

dealers who would exchange items for a pint! Joshua would collect almost anything second hand and scrap metal - although he was, not surprisingly, especially interested in gold coins. Eventually the business would have a dozen horses and carts and employ up to ten men collecting and sorting scrap and rags.

The hard work paid off; before long he owned most of the property between George Street and Lower Dagnall Street where scrap metal, antiques and old furniture piled up. Old Joshua was a well known figure around St Albans and people would flock to his yard to sell the scrap they had collected. The local streets echoed to the sound of horses hooves returning to George Street - more often than not the horses finding their own way to the yard as the drivers were frequently inebriated.

The 'Steptoe and Son' style business was run by Joshua with firm efficiency: everything was kept neat and tidy; he would strut around his yard in top hat

and frock coat carrying a length of metal with which he would check to see that the mounds of scrap were straight.

Joshua Pearce married Dorcas and had two sons: Joshua junior and Charles Henry. When Joshua senior died in 1910 at the age of 67 Joshua junior took over the business, storing furniture and metals at George Street whilst Charles set up on his own.

Charles Henry Pearce was born in 1868 and was as well known as his father old Joshua: He bought the Clock Tower shop and organised the renting out of space in the Clock Tower basement for refrigeration purposes, keeping meat and poultry there which were sold in the shop. His first wife Elizabeth ran the shop. Becoming a widower in his later years Charles married again.

As well as owning a shop, he was a dealer in antiques and recyclables, metals, rags, pelts and paper. Early in 1900 he started to recycle when he purchased wastepaper offcuts from Waterlows, Dunstable which were delivered to London Road railway station siding (which was linked to the present St Albans Abbey Flyer line) then carted to a Pearce yard for sorting and baling and delivered to John Dickinson by horse and cart ready for recycling. Rags and cotton would be taken to the premises on Lower Dagnall Street for sorting, it was here that the firm's first baling press was sited.

During the first world war the Company became the Hertfordshire area agent for the collection of rabbit skins.

In late 1918 Charles joined other local scrap dealers to go to France to collect scrap metal there. The consortium went out to the battlefields with a contract from the War Office to clear them of wrecked vehicles. Charles' son (Edgar) Eddie also brought back the scrap metal, but something on four wheels capable of moving was a challenge to him. Many of the unusable vehicles on the battlefields were given new life with massive transplants and several Pearce trucks soon appeared made up of odds and ends. According to family legend Eddie bought a revolver after crossing the Channel as 'you had to watch your stuff over there as the French would pinch anything'. Charles ran his Company until his death in 1923.

Edgar 'Eddie' took over the Company following his father's demise; during the second world war he was responsible for collecting scrap throughout

This page: *Different aspects of a bustling St Albans in the 1890s.*

Hertfordshire for the war effort. Eddie used premises in Albert Street where Pearce's Walk is now, Lower Dagnall Street, and Sopwell Nunnery Farm (where 'overspill' was sent from Albert Street in the 1920s) with an office in Verulam Road. He formed E Pearce & Sons in the 1940s when it amalgamated Joshua and Charles' businesses and continued the unbroken family tradition working as dealers in recyclables such as iron, steel, paper, bottles, pelts, rags and rabbit skins.

Opposite Sopwell Nunnery Farm was a family run dairy farm and allotments. Iron, metals and paper were stored near the nunnery ruins. The land was leased from the Gorhambury Estate belonging to the Grimstone family with the Earl of Verulam listed in the rent book. A half year's rent was £52 10s in those days. The land included tennis courts which were rented for £15 per annum to HA Richardsons, a local printing firm in the High Street, St Albans, next to Barclays Bank.

Older residents may just recall going through the narrow passage in George Street and walking through to Pearces' yard in Lower Dagnall Street where old rags and paper were collected. Ladies would sit in a circle supervised by the foreman, sorting out rags and throwing them into

sacks hanging in rows.

Eddie's sons Edgar and Jim (James) became involved in the firm in the late 1940s, moving the business to a five acre site, Acrewood Way, in the early 1960s.

They worked closely together, Edgar running the metal and textile side of the business and Jim the paper. But ordinary business continued at St Albans, with one major change since the war years - more and more cars were being brought in for scrap, to the annoyance of Eddie Pearce who considered them more of a nuisance than they were worth, since too much effort was expended stripping out accessories, windows and upholstery before they could be placed in the crushing machine to be compressed into cubes a couple of feet square. More economical were large factory contracts: sometimes a whole factory would be scrapped; a team from Pearces' once dismantled a

Top left: A baler from the 1930s. *Top right:* Arthur Bailey (standing), the longest serving employee, who stayed with the firm over 60 years, pictured during the second world war. *Above left:* A certificate awarded to Edgar Pearce to commemorate his membership of the Home Guard during World War II. *Above right:* A letter from the Ministry of Supply asking for double effort in collecting scrap iron and steel in the early 1950s. *Right:* The firm's weighbridge in Albert Street, in 1947.

whole chemical plant; the firm was well experienced in large projects and after the war had been involved in scrapping Lancaster bombers whilst a flotilla of steam rollers and other ancient vehicles would find their way to Pearces' yard. Iron and steel however were collected mainly from engineering factories as well as being bought from dealers. The firm was by now handling around 200 tons of iron and steel each week plus non-ferrous metals such as tin, silver, mercury, nickel and cadmium coming from the electrical and electronic industries.

Meanwhile the trade in rags, now known as textiles, still formed a lesser part of the business, with up to 60 per cent of every suit once being made from reprocessed material. Woollens and cottons were bought in from dealers, voluntary organisations and the public. A great deal of hand labour was involved in sorting rags with up to 130 grades of wool and many more grades of man-made fibres being identified. The biggest consumers for such materials were roofing felt manufacturers.

In 1965 E Pearce & Sons Ltd, by then employing some 70 people, went into partnership with J&J Maybank, the largest European Waste Paper Consortium, later becoming part of Reed International (who changed their company structure in the 1980s to Publishing and were

eventually no longer involved in paper making at Mills). The Partnership soon controlled over 30 per cent of Britain's wastepaper industry. By 1971 wastepaper pulping was already saving Britain importing £250 million worth of wood pulp each year. During this time Jim Pearce managed 6 waste paper reclamation centres throughout the Home Counties and East Anglia. The firm even had its own railway siding so that baled scrap metal and wastepaper could be taken straight from the yard and sent off to the foundries and reclamation factories. The Company was later contracted to remove part of this line!

Eddie Pearce died in 1969 having seen extraordinary changes in the firm. Jim and Edgar continued the growth with a new purpose-built warehouse which opened in Acrewood Way in 1971. It was designed to Jim's 'impossible' requirements by Richard Pearce, Joshua's son who was an Estate Agent, Surveyor and Architect in the district until the late 1980s. The warehouse increased working space by 12,000 square feet allowing an increase in output and turnover of 200 per cent.

The new £100,000 waste paper processing facility extended Pearces' existing wastepaper collection and baling activities with four new baling presses being installed. The factory also operated a bin collection system for customers' wastepaper, with skips supplied

Above: *Paperwork and ration coupons from the late 1940s.* **Below left:** *Jack (a Pearce Rep in 1948) and Helen Tolputt, Jim and Joan Pearce and Edgar and José Pearce at The Barn, St Albans.* **Below:** *Eddie Pearce.*

mated to form a group worth more than a million pounds. The Pearce company took over both the adjacent Hatfield Transport Ltd and Modern Disposals Ltd giving them a combined workforce of over 100.

Hatfield Transport was a general transport firm with a service workshop in which it was intended to maintain a 40 strong fleet of vehicles serving the whole group. Modern Disposals specialised in the removal of factory rubbish and local authority waste.

by Pearce hoisted on to lorries and unloaded beside floor level conveyor belts ready for immediate tipping.

The bin system offered customers several advantages, reducing labour charges for baling, reducing storage space for waste and allowed Pearces' to collect less frequently. Maintenance costs too were reduced, turn around of vehicles speeded up and work flowed more easily.

In the early 1970s three local companies amalga-

Above: Charles (Charlie) Pearce, Eddie's older brother, a musician, at the Plaza, Watford who helped at Albert Street during World War II. **Below and inset:** *The prize-giving ceremony for the Scouts Paper Chase in 1973.*

By the mid 1970s, in addition to wastepaper, Edgar was still arranging complete factory clearances including the dismantling of plant and machinery and was also accepting old cars and most domestic appliances at its depots. All metals were being accepted for recycling including brass, copper, aluminium, lead and zinc with off cuts and residual metals bought from builders, plumbers and electricians. And of course household rags and woollens were being bought for cash, including unsold jumble sale clothing.

1980 to manage the, then newly acquired, Luton Waste Paper; three years later he took over control of all the Group wastepaper activities under the title Pearce Recycling Company Limited. During the 1990s expansion continued with a basketfull of acquisitions including Portland Waste Paper, Security Destruction Ltd, (confidential papers) and Peterborough Waste. In the mid 1990s joint business ventures were launched with companies such as Secure Environmental Services, the Aylesford Paper Company and C Firbanks & Sons. In 1996 a second confidential waste facility was acquired in Norwich to add to those at Luton.

Recycling really began to take off in those years with soaring wastepaper prices providing a bonanza for charities. Early on Saturday mornings trucks, vans and cars would be queuing for a quarter of a mile outside Pearces' depot. Within a few hours more than a 100 tons of paper would have been off-loaded and money had changed hands - even before commercial disposers had begun unloading. Clubs, scout groups and even political parties were joining the paper chase to turn waste paper into cash for good causes. Charities were delighted as a national pulp shortage pushed prices far above anything which had been seen before: prices rose from £4.50 a ton to £20 per ton in a little over 15 months. More than £10,000 a year was being raised by scout groups alone and much more was promised.

By the mid 1990s more than three million tonnes of paper would be being recycled in Britain each year. A computerised weighbridge would weigh vehicles before and after deliveries and collections. Received waste was sorted into different grades before being transported by conveyor belt into the baling press where it was compressed into a block and tied with wire in a bale weighing three quarters of a tonne (this being done using one of the biggest balers in the world). The bales were then taken by lorry to paper mills where they were placed in gigantic vats containing water and chemicals to remove ink and glue. The washed paper was then squeezed between rollers and dried following which it was rolled into huge sheets ready for use.

During the 1980s industry and commerce changed dramatically. Metal foundaries closed and many publishing houses moved north to grant assisted areas to take the place of the closing steel mills. Pearce started to change into more of a service to industry and commerce instead of just recycling waste by-products from the manufacturing industry. Edgar set up Pearce Metals Ltd, in which he took no active part, with a site at the bottom of Holywell Hill. This firm is still trading today although the Pearce family no longer have an interest in it as Edgar retired as a director.

The current generation of the Pearce family is represented by Jim's son Simon who was first engaged in

*Top: A birds eye view of the yard in the 1970s. **Above:** Petrol coupons in use during the Suez Crisis in the early 1970s. **Right:** Opening the new warehouse in 1971.*

issue in the 1990s, with legislation and consequent expansion meant the firm acquired five more Confidential Waste plants. A partnership with Hays Business Service Group means that the Company has grown into the biggest Confidential Waste firm in the UK, with ten centres and a fleet of 105 lorries collecting 1,500 tonnes of confidential papers per week.

Every business must now show sound environmental policies. Today's rag and bone man must reflect and satisfy these requirements. On February 19th, 1997 after two years of market research, countless design proofs and many equipment prototype's, the Paper Planet recycling initiative was launched.

Recycled paper is now used to make stationery, tissues, packaging, newsprint and cardboard.

James (Jim) Pearce died in 1999, at nearly 73, after having been educated at Haileybury College and Cardiff University and later serving in the Royal Navy during the second world war. His lifetime's work was recycling and he was active in the local community being a founder member of St Albans Round Table. He later joined the 41 Club and the Rotary Club.

The concept of "Paper Planet" is a simple, one-stop shop of recycling solutions. Pearce customers, registered as members of the "Paper Planet" initiative are offered a total waste management and full recycling package along with assistance to meet their legal responsibilities. Paper, drinks cans, plastic cups, cardboard, newspapers and magazines, confidential documents, wooden pallets and toner cartridges are all collected and recycled under the Paper Planet initiative.

Today the Group has recycling facilities at St Albans, Corby, Luton and Milton Keynes. Materials are collected for sorting and baling from the Midlands, London across to Oxford and on to Cambridge.

Back at the Pearce Recycling operating centres, office paper is sorted and baled prior to being re-pulped for tissues, printing and writing papers. Drinks cans are sorted into either steel of aluminium and sold on to be smelted into

Over the past 70 years Pearce Recycling have built up a good market share within the sectors of printers and box makers, it's traditional customer base. Faced with the prospect of limited expansion and an ever declining Print Industry, the Pearce Recycling Management team under the guidance of Jim Pearce, highlighted a requirement to offer a full and comprehensive recycling programme to offices both large and small.

quality ingots, the largest of which can weigh 27 tonnes. These ingots are then sold all around the world for reuse as drinks cans or other metal based products. Plastic cups are sent away to be recycled into office consumables such as rulers and pencils. Wooden pallets are sorted into those fit for re-use and broken or unusable pallets. Those unfit for use are sent away to be shredded into chips suitable for walkways or to suppress weed growth in flower beds. Toner cartridges are refilled and sold back to business for re-use.

Furthermore, the Packaging regulations and Duty of Care Act place a legal obligation on today's Business to manage their waste in a professional and responsible manner. Data protection became an important

With this return to full recycling the present Management team are delighted to re-establish a direct link with the ideals of Charles Pearce some 100 years ago. In the early 1900s the Pearce family collected and recycled anything and everything.

Top left: *A Pearce truck doubles as Santa's sleigh for St Albans Round Table, 1971.* ***Above:*** *One of Pearce's paper collection lorries.*

Pearce Recycling along with Paper Planet intend to ensure that it's actions today will not adversely affect tomorrow's environment. In fact with the ongoing recycling and tree planting programmes, they intend to make a positive improvement for the future.

During the 1960s, 70s and 80s Pearce Recycling specialised in paper and board recycling. The Paper Planet initiative and its commitment to collect and recycle multi materials, brings the Pearce Group full circle for the new millennium.

Furthermore, Pearce Recycling are determined to take action today to save the environment of tomorrow. Therefore, part of Paper Planets' commitment to it's customers and the environment is to plant one tree for every 50 sacks of paper collected. To this end, the Company works closely with the Watling Chase Community Forest to identify suitable locations for tree planting. The Community Forests cover the whole of England and Wales and are responsible for increasing woodland cover from as little as 7 per cent to 30 per cent in some areas. The Paper Planet initiative has planted some 5,500 trees to date and intends to increase this figure year on year. Tomorrow's generations depend on our actions today.

The volume of material now handled by the group is far removed from the firm's modest origins: 3,500 tonnes of materials are recycled each week including paper, metal and plastics. The Security Division alone destroys 2,000 tonnes per week of which over 1,500 tonnes are in turn recycled. The range of materials sent for destruction includes paper, tapes, microfilm, credit cards and clothing. To achieve such volumes the Group has recently invested £2 million in plant, personnel and equipment. As a result the Group saves a quarter of a million trees every month.

Recycling has come a long way from the horse and cart. We might miss the sight and sound of the rag and bone man but at least we can be sure that his ancient calling is still flourishing, albeit as part of a new modern industry.

Top left: *Planting trees with local school children as part of the Paper Planet scheme introduced in 1997.*
Top right: *An aerial view of the premises.*
Left: *Jim and Simon Pearce with the Mayor of St Albans and members of the Charity Scheme.* ***Below:*** *Jim Pearce receiving the Quality Award from Kimberley Clark in the late 1990s.*

St Albans Central Library

Shopping spree

Before the imposing facade of the Town Hall is the expanse of the market place and St Peter's Street. There is no danger to the boys in short trousers as they pose for the camera. The mother, gently leading the child by the hand, has no need for the help of a crossing and a little green man. The horse waiting patiently for its owner as they unhurriedly shop, and the motorcycle abandoned in the middle have no fear of threat of being parked illegally. The horse trough, which stood where the lamppost and the mobile stall can be seen, was removed shortly after the cattle market was re-established in Drovers Way (which is now a multi-storey car park).

This scene changes on Saturdays when the market, which was introduced in Saxon times, is set up here. It has gradually expanded from the Market Place into St Peter's Street over the years.

The road surface appears to be made from loose material, although level and apparently in good condition.

At the top of the Street to the right of the Town Hall is the red brick Mansion House, with its balcony overlooking the Street. It is easy to imagine the Mayor standing on the balcony and addressing a crowd below.

How a cart as large as this one, with five spoked metal wheels at the front, and even cruder solid wheels at the back, is hauled into position below the clock is bewildering. It was certainly not designed for speed, or comfort. It would not go far with ease or with any thought for the noise that the rumbling wheels might make on the road surface. Straw was often scattered on the road in an attempt to deaden the sound. However, at ten minutes past eleven, business at the butcher's cart is brisk. The ladies are happily gossiping, again without concern about traffic. The horse drawn cart heading towards French Row poses no threat to them. Maybe the conversation is about the price of the meat, but probably not the unhygienic way in which it is displayed or served.

The archway opposite the Tower, used by the photographer to frame his picture, is all that remains of the Waxhouse. Abbott Wheathampstead rebuilt it from an earlier structure. Here candles and tapers were made and sold to pilgrims coming down this path, which is the shortest way for pedestrians to the Abbey and the shrine of St Alban. The Waxhouse stood until 1723 when all but the archway was demolished.

St Albans Central Library

The Morris car, like many of this era, was built on a chassis with the engine mounted in shafts at the front, very reminiscent of the shafts to which the horse had once been tethered. Its suspension and pneumatic tyres would have evened out the majority of lumps and bumps on the roads of the day. Although not yet possessing any form of heater, it offered a reasonable degree of comfort. That is more then can be said about the BSA

motorcycle parked behind it, with scissor action front girder suspension. Imagine the ride for the pillion passenger sitting on the square leather covered seat attached directly to the rear mudguard above the rear wheel where there was no suspension of any kind. The only protection from the spine-jarring ride was the pneumatic tyre. Many bicycles, like the ladies bicycle leaning against the tree, and motorcycles were made with machines originally used to produce guns, by such

companies as British Small Arms. At this time most people did not go out without some form of headwear and it is quite possible that the felt hats that can be seen, were made in St Albans. The gentleman, accompanying the lady with the pram, is sporting a very smart bowler hat. It seems a little worrying that the Foot Clinic is accessible through the entrance to 'True Form' shoe shop. The stalls seem to be doing a steady trade. They appear a little rickety, and must have

been difficult to manoeuvre into their positions with their wooden wheels with metal rims. Marks and Spencer shop stands on the spot where the County Club once stood. Behind it, accessed through a passageway where the sign 'stores' can be seen, was the County Theatre. The former actor Sidney Foster owned, and ran the theatre. It closed in 1932. The building, where 'Meakers' and 'True Form' are seen on this picture, was once a rather grand private house.

This impressive black and white timbered structure, part of which is occupied by W H Smith and Son, stands on the corner of Upper Dagnall Street. It has been considerably altered over the years. Heavy beams with several mortises cut in them can still be seen, which were probably an integral part of the earlier building. It was originally the Moot Hall. With the dissolution of the Abbey, this Town House was given to the Mayor and Chief Burgesses for use as a common hall. The upper floor became the courtroom, and the ground floor became the borough jail, and where the stocks and pillory were stored. The town court was summoned weekly by the ringing of a bell, and four jurors would be selected by the bailiff to try offenders. At a time when Craft Guilds flourished they would hold their meetings here. Around that time the Moot Hall would control the price and quality of bread and ale. It has also been called by different names such as Town Hall, Town House and various other titles. The town was now prosperous and, on the whole, self governing. When the Town Hall opened in 1831, the Moot Hall was sold by the council, who bought it back again in 1963. Despite the 'No Waiting' sign, the driver of the 'frog-eye' Sprite has parked to buy his newspaper. Whilst there is no risk of being caught by a traffic warden, the Bobby on his beat might well have something to say. The cobblestones across the road may be left over from the days when the road surfaces were muddy and such paths were necessary to keep shoes clean.

Making a living

The ladies working at Edwin Lees Boot and Shoe Factory in St Albans c1927, are fortunate in that their employment in this part of the country is relatively stable. Their working conditions seem pleasant in this well ventilated, sunny room.

The world seemed a wonderful place. According to an article written by Father Deagan of Coalville in the Illustrated Sunday Herald 1922, young ladies were at great moral risk through dancing to jazz music. He regarded their dresses as too loose, too airy, and too short. 'Fancy dress balls were not to be condemned, but there ought to be less fancy and more dress' he said.

Exciting things happened. Agatha Christie, as good as any of the mysteries she wrote, disappeared, and was eventually tracked down by her husband, to the Hydro Hotel in Harrogate, Yorkshire. Where she was reported to have been having a very pleasant time. What could be more romantic than a young, good looking American, who was daring enough to fly a small aeroplane across the Atlantic and land in Paris, thus winning a prize of twenty five thousand dollars? Only a few years ago the Suffragettes had won them the right to vote, but not until they were thirty. In 1928 the Equal Franchise Act came into operation allowing women the vote at the age of twenty-one the same as the men.

The men stand proudly displaying the shoes they have made, at Edwin Lees Boot and Shoe Factory in the late 1920s. They are fortunate to be in employment, as the number, who were not employed, never fell below one million during this period. On the 4th May 1926 there was silence in towns and cities throughout England. No buses or trains were moving. Only fifteen trains ran on London's Underground railway. It was a general strike. Newspapers reported that those who were fortunate enough to own cars, gave lifts to those who were trying to get around the city. The prosperity of Britain and America was an illusion to a large degree. Productivity was outstripping demand in the major industries. The illusion of prosperity lay in the fact that 'The Great Gatsby' people were extremely wealthy, but the majority were very poor. In places like Yorkshire, Scotland and Wales, where reliance was on textiles, mining, and the iron and steel industries, were beginning to feel the first effects of the slump, which began with the Wall Street crash on 24th October 1929. To these men it must have been a confusing time. Despite the apparent trouble looming, some people were very wealthy. George Bernard Shaw was offered the Nobel Prize for Literature, as they would no doubt have read in their newspapers. He had written accepting the prize, but turning down the award of six thousand five hundred pounds. This would seem like a vast sum to workers such as these. There was a happy announcement in 'The People' newspaper in1923. The Duke of York was to marry the lady Elizabeth, now better known to us all as the Queen Mother.

Left: Posing proudly in their National Fire Service Uniforms, these men of St Albans were a vital part of the Civil Defence. They had to be competent during the war years as a considerable number of incendiary bombs were dropped throughout Britain during the war years. The Auxiliary Fire Service was made up of volunteers who did this work in addition to their normal full-time work. When the National Fire Service was formed in 1941 many of the Auxiliary Volunteers joined. During the Blitz on London many of these men were drafted in to assist. St Albans was, to some minds, lucky, those bombs, which fell on them, were the ones left over from the raids on London, which the enemy aircraft had to drop in order to lighten the aircraft for the journey back. When it was realised that the lake in Verulamium Park offered them a good landmark by which to navigate, the council decided to have it drained. Emergency water tanks were built throughout the area because of this very real fear of incendiary devices. In 1940 there were two serious incidents of bombing. One fell on Camp Road, destroying three houses and killing four people. Not very far away there was a hospital. The second, about a week later, fell on a house in Beaumont Avenue, killing another four people. Other bombs fell in less dangerous places like the Verulamium Playing Fields. Many people had 'Morrison' shelters. These were small steel cages about the size of a table, for which purpose they were often used. They were strong enough to support the weight of falling debris, or a collapsed building, should the house take a direct hit.

Below: If there was any good in war it was that it made people ask, 'What are we fighting for?' There was an expectation that conditions in the home and at work must improve. The war at changed attitudes towards social class, as bombs fell on rich as well as poor. The hard fought freedom for the right of free speech filtered through. People demanded better conditions and a reasonable pay. Identity cards were scrapped in 1952, and in the same year King George VI died. Queen Elizabeth II was crowned and the country watched the Coronation on small purple tinted television screens. Neighbours were invited in to watch if they didn't possess a television. All children were given a copy of the New Testament with an inscribed cover, and a transfer printed mug. Many of the mugs did not arrive home from school in one piece, probably increasing their value for future collectors.

There had been many changes made during the early 1900s, children received regular medical inspections in their schools, and the local authorities had to provide them with a school dinner. Without school dinners, there would be nothing for young boys and music hall comedians to make jokes about. Children themselves might not have seen these moves as 'progress' when the mobile dental surgery arrived in the school playground. Many feared the disgrace of being discovered to be infested by head lice. Everyone dreaded the 'nit nurse'. School was now inflicted on them up to the age of fifteen because of the ideas of a man in the government called Aneurin Bevan.

Two brothers, one of whom can be seen on the front row, between the two gentlemen wearing spectacles, founded the Ballito factory. His name was Mr C Kotzin. The firm opened as a small private business, established by the two brothers. At first they imported cheap American hose. They provided a good service and soon commanded respect within their trade. Their reputation and sales grew swiftly. When, in 1925, import duties made it possible to produce silk and artificial silk hosiery on a competitive basis. It was the first mass production of pure silk stockings in this country. Sales grew and new premises were sought. Fleetville area gained its curious name when Smith's printing works left Fleet Street and set up

its works on the outskirts of St Albans. It stood on the corner of Hatfield Road and Sutton Road, where there is now a supermarket. The city was steadily expanding in that direction. They called their printing works 'Fleetville', and soon the area became known by the same name. The building was enlarged and became the first home of Ballito in St Albans. American technicians were brought over and a new home industry was born. By 1929 it was a huge success. Orders for their product came in from every part of the country. This period of prosperity carried the company through the depression of the 1930s. A new public company was formed and within a few hours it was oversubscribed. A large oak had grown from a little acorn.

This page and overleaf: 'Pretty maids all in a row,' the girls from the Ballito factory pose in this uncomfortable workroom. The light blocked out because of the blackout regulations. Extra lights strung from the ceiling in rows. Yet all of these ladies, despite the hardships of the years of austerity and rationing, worked hard to make their contribution to the war's end. They combed their hair in the styles of the stars, and dreamed that they, like Vivien Leigh, would be whisked away by Rhett Butler in the same way as he did with Scarlet O'Hara, in 'Gone With the Wind'. They needed to be able to escape into this romantic world, after working all day in a hot factory. After work they could always bath with Lifebuoy Toilet soap, which promised, 'It'll soon put new life back into you'. The war effort needed a healthy workforce, and, if possible, a happy one. Music was encouraged in the work place, and we hummed and danced to the music of Glenn Miller, Anne Shelton and others. The government launched campaigns to educate the workers in ways of keeping healthy. They warned that, 'Coughs and sneezes spread diseases'. We were told to, 'Trap your germs in a handkerchief'. The songs of Vera Lynn were optimistic, romantic, and contained messages that were comforting to hear, like,' We'll meet again'. They worked to the music of Charlie Kunz as his fingers played his piano medleys.

From previous page: Ted Ray made them laugh, and so did Flanagan and Allen. They became skilled in making their own cloths from remnants, blackout curtain material, and anything they could get their hands on. They made underwear from parachute silk. There seemed no end to their ingenuity. Trousers became fashionable, although practical there are none in evidence at the Ballito factory. They are all wearing the overalls provided by the firm. The

oily floors made clogs and heavy shoes the only sensible footwear. The Ballito factory kept up production of stockings as well as helping with the war effort. Newspapers reported they were surprised to find that, to the ladies, the lack of silk stockings was more of a threat than poison gas. They could 'mend and make do', as the government urged them to do, where coats and other clothes were involved, but there was no way of 'making do and mending' their stockings.

Left: The continued success meant that, in 1935, drastic reorganisation within the mills was necessary. Every department was enlarged and yet more machines installed to keep pace with the constant rise in demand for their quality products. The new machines were housed in the new building, adjoining the old, in Sutton Road.
New fifty-one gauge, and forty-five gauge knitting machines were soon increasing productivity. Output had risen by fifty per cent before the building of the extension was completed. In the following year the latest type of seamless knitting machines were added, with the proportionate looping, seaming and other machines to support them. The woman in the picture is working at one of the looping machines. Further expansion continued up to 1939. By now though the threat of war was becoming very real. New words were entering our vocabulary. 'Conscription' was one of them. Perhaps it is in the mind of the lady as she conscientiously works the looping machine. Or possibly her mind is simply on the last film by the handsome heartthrob, Clark Gable. At least the stability of the company through difficult times meant that her thoughts could be of lighter matters than unemployment and poverty. She could be comforted to so degree by the knowledge that the management, with continued foresight, had provided a fully equipped air-raid shelter when they built the new factory. In 1939 the people were introduced to the sound of the 'Enemy Approaching' siren, and the welcomer 'All Clear'.

Above: The poster, which is receiving the finishing touches, will no doubt create a great deal of interest for the ladies who lived during, or just after the war. They had been taught to 'Make Do and Mend' through the government's campaign. Clothes were rationed from June 1941 and points were allocated. Everyone had a clothing allowance book. Initially everyone had 66 coupons per year, but this was reduced to 48 in the Spring of 1942. A ladies dress required eleven coupons. A coat, eighteen, and a pair of men's trousers used eight of the coupons. Each item of clothing was carefully worked out on a sliding scale. 'Make Do and Mend' exhibitions were given at local stores. W S Green's of Chequer Street advertised that an expert needlewoman would be demonstrating in the store every day for a week. These 'austerity' regulations brought about changes in fashion design. Because of the scarcity of material, skirts became shorter; the number of pockets and pleats on garments was reduced. Turn-ups on trousers disappeared. Some ingenious ideas came from the adapting and changing of clothes. Stockings were not always easy to get, even though the Ballito factory had made its home in St Albans. Many young ladies, who lived during these years, will remember painting their legs with all manner of things to try to give the appearance that they were wearing stockings. It was not unheard of for them to use gravy browning to colour their legs, and an eyebrow pencil to draw a line up the back to give the illusion of a seam. Maybe the line on the backs of their legs did look like a seam, in a dance hall lit only by spotlights reflecting off a rotating ball covered in small square mirrors.

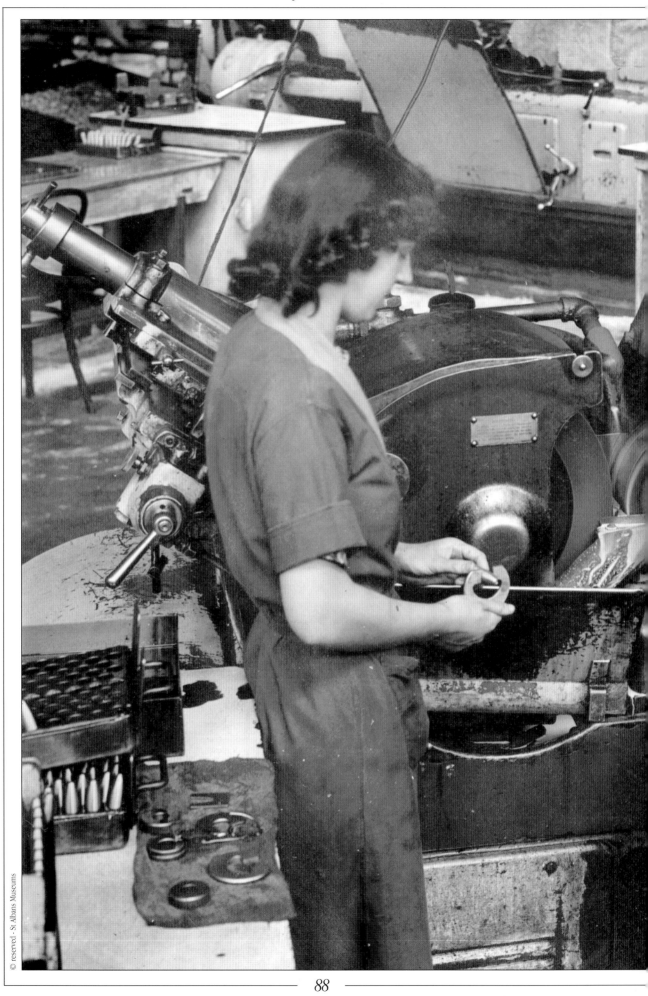

This photograph shows clearly the size and weight of some of the machines that were pushed and shoved into place, after the sewing machines had gone. The effort and organisation needed ranks alongside that of the building of the pyramids. The use of a micrometer for measuring is a far cry from the work that had been undertaken earlier in this place.

Large numbers of women were drafted into war work. The first to be conscripted in this way were unmarried women between the ages of thirty and forty, but in the summer of 1943, all women who did not have children under the age of fourteen, were told they must do war work. The government had a shock when they were placed in the position of having to provide nursery facilities because so many women had volunteered to do the work. Attitudes towards women in work were forever changed. Although many men joined the armed forces, there were some in occupations that were exempt because they were considered essential. These were called 'reserved' occupations. In the beginning they could volunteer to join the armed forces if they so wished. In some cases so many had joined up that the government decided to place the work under an 'Essential Work Order'. This meant those doing the work could not be sacked, neither could they leave their job even if they wanted to.

So many miners chose to join the army, rather than work down in the pits, that coal production was seriously affected. Ernest Bevin came up with a very unpopular idea. One in every ten men conscripted would have to work in the mines. It was not well received. They were given the nickname 'Bevin Boys'. Only recently has their contribution to the war been fully recognised. There were no medals for them at the end of the war, and very few other benefits.

We would imagine that this work was not without an element of danger for these women making the final inspections of the Oerlikon ammunition shells. It was certainly not without discomfort. This room was always referred to as 'the cage'. Ballito, like many other factories, boarded up its windows in order to achieve total blackout. The laws were strict and rigidly applied. It was assumed that the enemy would attack at night so every light from every home, vehicle, street lamp, and public building, and. Of course, a factory like this one, had to be hidden. Ballito, like many other factories boarded up its windows, rather than covering them with the black material used in homes and other places. The regulations were very strictly applied and not even the smallest chink of light must show.

Consequently windows could not be opened to provide ventilation or light. It was hot and uncomfortable working in the cage under artificial light. To help to carry the workers through this difficult time the radio played many music and quiz programmes. 'Music while you work', everyone who lived at the time can sing these words to the tune, but naughty rhymes about Hitler and his colleagues were also added, after all, they would have argued, he is the one responsible for all this, and they worked a little harder because they knew that the end would come quicker if they did. They laughed at the gentle questioning of Wilfred Pickles as he tried to elicit an answer from a contestant who he, and the rest of the country would be happy to see succeed. 'Twenty Questions', was the programme in which Violet was always asked to 'give them the money'.

The experience of having to train large numbers of people new skills, which the management of Ballito had gained when they first arrived in St Albans, must have served them well when they had to once more retrain their workforce to face the new task, and acquire the necessary new skills. There would be many adjustments to make. The factory was no longer the spotlessly clean place it had been, and many found that clogs were the best footwear for the oily floors. The noises and smells would have been unfamiliar. The machines certainly were. The move from a looping machine in the manufacture of stockings to the use of a lathe for turning shell cases is a large leap to take. The managers said that they had come from all departments, to join in a new comradeship. They had confidence in one another and assured of returning to their old jobs in better days. Their former skills would not be forgotten. After the war many did find, however, that they had become comfortable with their new abilities, and the move back required more adjustment that had been anticipated.

The girl at the lathe is turning the nose of a shell, whilst her colleague is measuring the length of the 20 mm Oerlikon projectile. What looks like a bracelet around her wrist does not seem like a sensible thing to wear when operating the lathe, but maybe she is simply posing for the camera, and will be removing it before the shaft begins to turn.

ballito STOCKINGS **NATIONALLY KNOWN**

Our products became popular very rapidly, the result of good publicity <u>and</u> good service to the public.
"Mr Charles Kotzin has been the power behind ballito's advertising, inaugurating many novel ideas, many topical and interesting campaigns.

During the war, these ballito "Reminder" Ear Spaces have been seen in most National papers. This was due to the foresight of Mr Charles Kotzin in booking these spaces two or three years before the war.

ballito have been progressive, too, with selling ideas to retailers — specialized packings, shops-within-shops, and a great variety of window display material.

ballito ON THE AIR
ballito were the largest radio advertisers for years culminating in our famous Tango advertising scheme — one of the greatest publicity campaigns ever promoted

Left: On the first of September 1939, Hitler's army invaded Poland. Britain issued an ultimatum that, if they did not leave Poland, a state of war would exist between Britain and Germany. The ultimatum expired at 11 am on Sunday 3 September. The people waited breathlessly by their radios for an announcement by the Prime Minister Neville Chamberlain. At 11.15 am he told the nation that he had received no such undertaking and, therefore, this country was at war with Germany. From that time the whole of industry was geared to the war effort. Ballito factory was no different, and, with the same planning and good management as well as the willingness of the workforce, they quickly changed from producing stockings to producing Oerlikon ammunition shells. There was a determination and willingness as they faced the task of this formidable change over. Lighting, benches, bins and racks were removed, and over three hundred sewing machines, with a similar number of seaming and looping machines, had to be dismantled and cleared to make way for the huge American machines. These machines arrived before this task had been accomplished. Many of them were massive automatic lathes. They weighed over eleven tons each. They were manhandled into positions already planned for them and connected to power without any delay. It was a lesson in cooperation and good planning. Everyone hoped that this effort would contribute to bringing about a quick conclusion to the war.

Above: We have to admire the drive and innovation of Mr Charles Kotzin. To have had the ability to inspire and drive his workers in the way that he obviously did from the success of the company, has to be admired. His poster justifiably boasts that their product became popular rapidly because of good publicity. He makes his company personal by introducing himself, and tells the public how clever they were to think of all the different ways that they have used to bring their product to the attention of the public. The 'reminder' spaces in newspapers were booked two or three years before the war. Little wonder that he can boast of 'foresight'. He saw the potential power of the radio as an advertising tool. How smart of him to realise that the offer of 'luxury', and 'glamour' would be irresistible to ladies who had lived through the years of austerity. Which woman wouldn't want 'Lasting Loveliness', or 'Slender Silken ankles' It must have seemed about time that they had the opportunity of a little 'Luxury'. Mr Kotzin had the power to give them all these things. Ballito stockings could be with, or without, seams. Superfine so that it was they, and not the stockings, who were beautiful. Notice the care with which the packaging is designed, that skill was passed on to the retailer through assistance with window displays. The idea of 'shops within shops' seems a modern idea, but Ballito appear to have pioneered the concept. In the words of the poster, 'inaugurating many new ideas'.

A thousand years of schooling

What do Nicholas Breakspeare, England's only Pope, lyricist Sir Tim Rice and Professor of Mathematics Stephen Hawking all have in common? The answer is that all three were once students at St Albans School.

Few schools occupy such historic buildings or such an important site as the St Albans School. That there was a school associated with the Abbey by 1100 there is no doubt; that it existed very much earlier than this, perhaps from soon after the foundation of the monastery is a reasonable assumption. AD 948, the year of Abbot Wulsin's foundation of the parishes of St Michael, St Peter and St Stephen, has been taken as the likeliest date for the School's foundation.

The School crest unites the coat of arms of Sir Nicholas Bacon with the family motto of Abbot Geoffrey de Gorham, linking two of the School's greatest benefactors. The School's Latin motto Non Nobis Nati means 'Born not for ourselves'. The motto embodies the School's idea of social responsibility and service to the community and a recognition that privilege must be balanced with responsibility.

Geoffrey de Gorham became associated with the School around 1100 after the then Abbot had asked for the renowned Norman scholar to be sent for. Nineteen years later Geoffrey de Gorham was elected Abbot himself. By the end of the twelfth century the School would be described as 'such that there would be hardly be found in

Above: A cricket match in the early 1900s.
Below: The Gateway around 1890, showing the Headmaster's House to which an additional storey had recently been added.

charter granted the right for two persons in the town to keep a tavern and sell wine - the fee for granting the charter to be used to support a school. Fascinatingly, funding via these wine licences would continue until 1922.

Today School hours are 8.40am to 4pm: in 1570 the hours for the School's 120 scholars were a less welcome 6am to 5pm in summer and 7am to 5pm. Until 1602 there were no fees though parents were expected to provide amongst other things, ink, paper, pens, candles and a bow, three arrows and a shooting glove.

The School flourished for the next century or so. A low point for the School however came in 1762 when Benjamin Preedy, Master of the School, reported to the Mayor and Burgesses that he had no pupils to teach. Part of the problem had been a

England a better or more fruitful or more useful or giving greater opportunity to its scholars'.

By 1300 the School was located on or near the site of the present Romeland House and continued there, controlled by the Abbey, until Henry VIII's dissolution of the monasteries in 1539.

Ten years after King Hal's reorganisations the Abbey's last Abbot Richard Borman was granted a private Act of Parliament by Henry's successor the young Edward VI to establish a grammar school in the Lady Chapel, whilst in 1553 a Royal Charter gave the Mayor and Burgesses the right to maintain a grammar school. Both Borman's and the towns attempts at re-establishing the School seem to have been unsuccessful until 1570 when Sir Nicholas Bacon, Lord Keeper of the Great Seal obtained a 'wine charter' from Elizabeth the First. The wine

Above: The old School Hall. **Top:** *One of the classes in the early part of the 20th century.* **Right:** *The Science Block before extensive alterations in the 1950s.*

lack of investment and the profligacy of the Mayor and Burgesses spending funds on their own entertainment. Another explanation for the School's lack of appeal was that it taught only Latin and Greek.

In fact, because of the School's founding charter, until 1845 nothing but Latin and Greek could be taught at St Albans. In that year a new charter was introduced enabling the syllabus to be extended and to allow boarders to be officially taken for the first time. The School, went through a revival under the Mastership of Henry Hall between 1845 and 1863. Sadly, the revival was short-lived and by 1871, when the School left the Lady Chapel to move to the Abbey Gatehouse, there were fewer than ten boys on the roll.

The Great Gatehouse had been used for many purposes previously: it had been courthouse and most recently a prison. An appeal committee raised the £1,100 needed to buy the building and the School moved in with pupil numbers gradually rising towards a hundred by 1880. Things were improving, and by 1886 an extension was built to provide boarding accommodation whilst in 1892 a chemical laboratory and a lecture room were constructed .

It was around this time that organised games started: cricket and football being played on a meadow in Holywell Hill although games seem to have done little to attract new students with numbers down to only 67 by 1901.

It would take until 1931 to build up student numbers to a healthy 450 boys. That growth and increasing reputation was in the main due to the efforts of E Montague-Jones who was appointed Headmaster in 1902 and would stay in post for

*Above centre: The School crest. **Top right:** An aerial view of the School in the early 1960s. **Top left:** The Science School after the 1950s extension.*

almost 30 years apart from a year's service in France during the Great War.

Increasing numbers of boys meant a need to increase accommodation: in 1907 Old Hall or School Hall with eight classrooms was built, whilst in 1911 School House with accommodation for the Headmaster, his family and more than 30 boarders was opened.

The word 'Grammar' had incidentally been dropped from the School's name in the early years of the 20th century and its public school status made clear by a switch from soccer to 'rugger' in 1919.

In 1928 bvb a new block of four classrooms had to be built at the southern end of the School yard connected by the 'Bridge of Sighs' to the Hall. Such growth continued throughout the next decade with, most significantly, the opening of a new science block in 1936, a brick and ferro-cement structure designed by Percy Blow. The following year the School was able to buy the 'Hat Factory' a two storey building behind 9 Fishpool Street and used by the School's cadet corps including the installation of a rifle range.

Such training would be necessary: on the eve of the second world war student numbers stood at around 500. Many of those would soon be using their cadet training in a real war. And many would give their lives for their country as had their predecessors in

New Hall was opened together with the Pen Arthur Field Studies Centre in the Brecon Beacons national park - then a derelict hill farm cottage and now fully restored and used for field trips and study weekends.

The final quarter of the twentieth century began with the opening of a new science wing and technical centre whilst in 1975 the direct grant system was abolished and the School reverted to full independence.

In 1987 the science block was extended with new classrooms and a technology suite was built. In the Old Hall a New Library was created on the upper floor.

Perhaps however the most significant change in the School's thousand year history came in 1991 when girls were admitted to the sixth form for the first time. That same year the Playing Field Trust bought the 400 acre Cheapside Farm on which the Woollam playing fields would be finally developed in

the first world war. The Old Albanian dead of both wars are commemorated in the School war memorial and the wall panels next to it.

Following the war's end sports facilities were at the forefront of development: in 1947 the King Harry Playing fields were leased from Lord Verulam - a descendant of Sir Nicholas Bacon whilst the following year the Orchard tennis courts were opened.

And in the mid 1950s a new gymnasium block was opened. By the 1950s student numbers had risen to 650 with a three form entry. Boarding was a worry and the space occupied by the relatively few boarders could be used for other purposes. In 1957 boarding ceased.

During the decade of the 1960s developments continued with the building by staff and pupils of an open air theatre; more significantly, in 1968, the

2000. Despite continuing emphasis on science, the arts had not been forgotten, and in 1994 new Art Studios were opened followed four years later by the building of new laboratories and the whole School site being networked for computers in 1998.

St Albans School is one of Europe's most ancient educational establishments. Today its unique atmosphere blends the historic with the ultra-modern and provides a 21st century education which encompasses not just the academic but also the principles of the School motto by giving service to others.

Top left: Rugby, just one of the major team games enjoyed by pupils at the School. *Above:* Music is an option available to all School pupils. *Right:* The current Headmaster, Andrew Grant.

Building a reputation

The St Albans firm of builders, contractors and decorators, C&S Dumpleton Ltd based in Culver Road, is now more than a hundred years old having been founded in 1900 by Charles William Dumpleton. Since then four more generations have been involved in the business.

Charles William was followed by his sons Charles and Sidney who along with their sister Edith Peters saw the company through the difficult years of the second world war. Later Sidney's son John and daughter Betty Latchford joined the firm along with their cousin Roy Christmas. John's son Graham, his wife Sharon and general manager William Chasen guided the company through to the millennium, with the next generation, Graham's son Gary, now general foreman.

CW Dumpleton ran his business from premises at 54 Victoria Street. Those first premises were used until 1932. Late in 1900 however a yard had been bought at nearby Culver Road from where the firm still trades today, with large workshops and an office eventually being built there.
At the outset all joinery was produced using hand tools,

wooden scaffolding was still the norm and transport was horse drawn wagons. In the day before the first world war the firm's joiners were allowed to drink beer at their work benches - though they were not allowed to smoke as the wood shavings which were knee deep to keep their feet warm were a fire hazard. Many real characters were employed: one of the firm's maintenance men was an ex sergeant major who had fought a battle at the Khyber Pass.

The business was incorporated only in 1935 with the company taking its name from the two brothers Charles and Sidney.

During the second world war when many tradesmen were called up the yard was designated a first aid station and as an air raid observation post.

With its unusual name C&S Dumpleton Ltd is a firm easily remembered in the trade. And as more clients seek the reassurance that can only come with the knowledge that one is dealing with a long-established firm few can offer such an outstanding and distinguished record.

Above: *Company founder, Charles William Dumpleton.*
Below: *An early letterhead.*

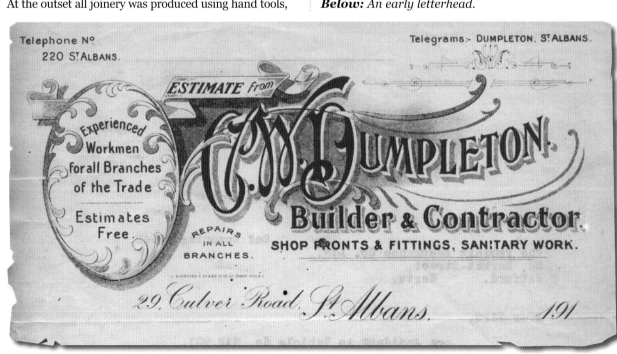

Providing a sound education

St Albans High School is an independent day school for 800 girls between the ages of four and eighteen. Whilst retaining close links with the Diocese of St Albans, Christian teaching is based on the doctrine of the Church of England but it is by no means exclusively Anglican and girls from all religious denominations and faiths are welcome.

The girls from the High School have been a familiar sight to residents of St Albans since the school's foundation in 1889. The school opened on Thursday 2nd May with its first headmistress being Anna Grace Lee a Cambridge-educated mathematics scholar.

The first school building was the old dispensary on the corner of Holywell Hill and Albert Street, a site which had once been occupied by the Old Crown Inn.

A building in London Road was acquired in September 1889 for a kindergarten and preparatory school and in January 1890 the Kindergarten had moved to 31 Holywell Hill, the seniors occupying the old dispensary.

Surprisingly uniforms were not the norm in those early days - except for 'drill' when gym tunics and black stockings were worn.

By 1901 the pupil roll had reached 64 and five years later 80. At that time new premises were sought and in 1907 Townsend House on the Hall Place estate became empty and was demolished.

Above: *A portrait of Miss Archibald, painted by Harold Knight, RA in 1951.* **Right:** *The 1912 Tennis team.* **Below:** *Some of the Sixth Form pictured in 1926.* **Bottom:** *The Kindergarten in 1927.*

St Albans High School for Girls Ltd bought some of the land and built a Queen Ann style school large enough for 200 pupils - the present main building.
The new school building opened in September 1908 standing in its own grounds which included a basket ball ground and playing fields for which the by now 146 pupils were no doubt grateful. The number of boarders began to increase and the school was able to buy Bricket House between Upper Marlborough Road and Bricket Road as a boarding house. A cottage was soon opened in the grounds of Bricket House and fitted out for Domestic Science - although there was a considerable and surprisingly modern sounding debate at the time about whether such a non-academic subject was as valuable to girls as sciences and languages.

During the first year of the Great War the school building was requisitioned to house the First London Irish Regiment and schoolwork was transferred to the museum in Hatfield Road, whilst science lessons were

Above: Girls in the Parr Observatory in 1937.
Top: Girls gardening for the inter-house competition in 1926. *Right:* The school hall in 1969. The Oakdene Library is now sited where the hall used to be.

conducted at the St Albans Grammar School. By late 1915 however the soldiers had moved out and pupils returned.

It was in 1921 that the house system was first introduced: Julian, Mandeville, Paris and Verulam. Julian is named after Juliana de Berners, prioress of Sopwell Nunnery who wrote the 'Boke of St Albans'. Mandeville is named after the traveller Sir John Mandeville said to be buried at the Abbey; Paris after the historian of St Albans Abbey, Matthew Paris and Verulam after Lord Verulam, Francis Bacon.

An official playing field was opened in 1927, bought next to the school for £1,066, an event coinciding with the opening of a new wing to house the preparatory school.

The death of George V in 1936 coincided with another stage of development when new science labs were formally opened together with a new library and an observatory built below the gym. Two years later the school acquired 'Podhu' a house in Townsend Drive subsequently known as Glossop House and later still as Library House.

The outbreak of the second world war in 1939 led to inevitable changes: cellars at Boro'gate, the senior boarding house acquired in 1928, were used for shelters and a trench dug in the school grounds. Some confusion was caused in the first days of the war when

Parliament Hill LCC Girls school was evacuated by mistake to St Albans and the High School took its part in finding accommodation and facilities for the evacuees.

Following the war's end an additional house, Kingsley, at the end of Townsend Avenue, was acquired in 1950 and boarders transferred from Glossop House which would then become the school library.

Trinity Term 1961 saw the beginning of work on the site of Archibald House where a new wing was to be built containing a dining room, a kitchen, a form room and Bursar's office; six years later £35,000 was raised to build two new laboratories and a new preparatory building.

By 1970 the pupil roll had reached 310 in the senior school and 200 in the junior, four years later a decision by the Governors would lead to the closing in stages of the kindergarten and transition departments to make more

room for older pupils for which there was greater demand. This proved an effective policy and by 1974 there were 601 girls in the school including 194 in the junior department, the kindergarten having closed in 1972.

Teaching staff numbers had reached 30 full time and 13 part time teachers in the senior school and 8 full time and 2 part time in the junior school.

Growth in numbers led in turn to a demand for more accommodation; £150,000 was needed and soon raised to house a sixth form common room and tutorial rooms as well as geography and needlework rooms. In 1981 the first computer was bought with the help of a government grant.

In the 1980s it was clear that new science and technology labs were needed as well as computer rooms thus a design technology centre came into being between the art and science departments and the opening of a new sciences and technology block in May 1986.

The 1990s saw the opening of the new sports hall on the site of the tennis courts by the swimming pool and five new classrooms, IT room and laboratory in the Junior House replacing wooden huts that had been used for 40 years. The Oakdene Library was sited in the area used as the original school hall and the Du Cane Drama Studio was built next to the music school in Ringwood.

Any school is however far more than just its buildings: it is the pupils and staff which make a school. St Albans High School today continues the tradition established at the time of its foundation, providing the highest standards of academic education together with excellent sports and music facilities within an ethos of social responsibility.

Having progressed from its small beginnings at the end of the 19th century, today the school aims to give each girl the stimulus and encouragement to develop her academic abilities, a wide range of interests and a sense of personal values. Quite what the first headmistress, Anna Lee, would have made of the school today one can only imagine. She would no doubt be astonished at the number of pupils, the size of the buildings and modern technology - but she would surely recognise the commitment of the school to providing every girl with a forward looking, dynamic education.

Top left: *The school in 1978.* ***Above left:*** *Pupils in the Junior School.* ***Left:*** *An art lesson.*
Below: *Governors and VIPs celebrate the school's centenary in 1989.*

Holywell Hill has always been busy as it is part of the London to Holyhead Road

Acknowledgments

St Albans Central Library
All photographs with the following endorsement '© reserved - St Albans Museums' are
copyright reserved and reproduced by kind permission of St Albans Museums
Eileen Hedges
Beryl Houseley
Anne Wheeler

Thanks are also due to
John Thornton who penned the editorial text and
Steve Ainsworth for his copywriting skills